Sunday Savers™

Choose the Right—A, Ages 4-7

Fun activities that
correlate with the
Primary 2
CTR-A
manual lessons
with Thought Treats

Use for Primary lessons and
family home evening to
enhance learning

You'll Find: A-Z Topics
to Match Primary Lessons

Atonement   Baptism   Birth of Jesus   Blessings

Child of God   Choosing the Right   Church   Christmas   Easter

Example   Families   Forgiveness   Follow Jesus   Gratitude

Happiness   Holy Ghost   Jesus   Kindness   Laws   Love

Love Others   Missionary   Obedience   Peacemaker   Prayer

Priesthood   Priesthood Blessings   Reverence   Sabbath

Sacrament   Second Coming   Service   Sharing   Talents

Teaching Treasures   Temptations   Thank-you   Tithing   Truth

Introducing the Author and Illustrator, Creators of

The Following Series of Books and Printable CD-ROM Versions of Each Book

- **PRIMARY LESSON ACTIVITIES & HANDOUTS** (for manuals 1–7 & more): SUNDAY SAVERS Nursery, Sunbeams, CTR-A and CTR-B (ages 4-7); Book of Mormon, D&C, New Testament, and Old Testament (ages 8-11); Faith-in-God We Love Activity Days and Super Activity Days and Socials (girls 8-11)

- **CURRENT SHARING TIME:** SUNDAY SAVERS Sharing Fun, Sharing Fun Treasures, and Singing Fun

- **GAMES & ACTIVITIES FOR FAMILY HOME EVENING & PRIMARY** (colored to tear out and use): Fun in a Flash, Tons of Fun, Jesus Loves Me, and Funner than Fun Gospel Games

  FHE Books with CD-ROM to print images in black-and-white or color: SHORT & SWEET with a Treat (52 Family Home Evenings), Gospel Games, and Gospel Fun Activities

- **SINGING** (colored & ready to use) Series: Super Little Singers, Super Singing Activities, and Singing Fun (above)

- **YOUNG WOMEN:** Young Women Fun-Tastic! Activities: Lesson Lifesavers for manuals 1–3 and Young Women Fun-tastic! Personal Progress Motivators

Mary Ross, Author

Mary Ross is an energetic mother and has been a Primary teacher and Relief Society president. She loves to help children and Young Women have a good time while learning. She has studied acting, voice, and modeling. Her varied interests include writing, creating activities and children's parties, and cooking. Mary and her husband, Paul, have a daughter. They live in Lehi, Utah.

Jennette Guymon-King, Illustrator

Jennette Guymon-King studied graphic arts and illustration at Utah Valley State College and the University of Utah. She served a mission in Japan. She enjoys sports, reading, cooking, art, gardening, and freelance illustrating. Jennette and her husband, Clayton, live in Bluffdale, Utah. They are the proud parents of daughters Kayla Mae and Shelby, and sons Levi and Carson.

Copyright © 2011 by Mary H. Ross and Jennette Guymon-King - All Rights Reserved
Covenant Communications, Inc., American Fork, Utah, Printed in the United States of America

Sunday Savers™ Choose the Right-A, Ages 4-7
ISBN 978-1-60861-845-3
ACKNOWLEDGMENTS: Thanks to www.creativedelights.com lettering delights for use of fonts for some activities.

Introduction

Sunday Savers™ CTR-A contains visuals, crafts, games, handouts, and activities that match every lesson in the Primary 2 CTR-A manual. Simply find the lesson in the manual or on the Internet at lds.org. Then copy the visuals in this book, or print them from the CD-ROM in color or black-and-white (sold separately, shown right, and on the back cover of this book).

Sunday Savers activities are teaching tools to reinforce gospel messages in the manual. Since "a picture is worth a thousand words," use these visuals to help children get the most out of lessons in both family home evening and Primary.

HOW TO USE THIS BOOK

- You will find two tables of contents in this book: one A-Z to help you spot gospel subjects and visuals quickly, and one listed by lessons 1-47 to help you find week-to-week lesson activities.
- Each activity/visual in this book correlates with specific parts of the lesson (see the PREPARATION section). When there is time left after the lesson, you'll have something fun to do, or you can use the visuals to help you teach the lesson concepts.
- You'll also find a THOUGHT TREAT to match each lesson (when appropriate).
- Copy lessons ahead of time and gather supplies to avoid last-minute preparation. Supplies needed: Include scissors, tape, glue, crayons, zip-close plastic bags, lunch-size sacks, hole punch, yarn or ribbon, string, wooden craft sticks, metal brads, and safety pins.

• REVERENCE RACCOON CHART. Reward children for reverence (or discourage the lack of it) by copying a Reverence Raccoon Chart and set of raccoon glue-on stickers (in the back of this book, shown left) for each child. When children are reverent during the lesson, reward them with a raccoon sticker they can glue on their chart (weeks 1-46). If they are not as reverent as they should be, don't give them a raccoon (or cut a raccoon in half). The next week when they see their chart, they are reminded to be reverent in Heavenly Father's house so they can earn a raccoon on their chart. If they are extra reverent give them the other half of the raccoon they didn't earn the week before.

• CTR TESTIMONY TREASURE BOX. Create this box to store classroom creations. You'll need the following: a copy of box label and glue-on stickers; and a parent's note (found in the back of this book); a shoe or shirt box for each child; and scissors, glue, contact paper, and crayons. To make box: (1) Cover box with contact paper. (2) Color and cut out box label and box stickers. (3) Glue label and stickers on box. (4) Glue parent's note inside lid.

TM

TABLE OF CONTENTS #1 (1-46 Lesson Subjects & Activities for Primary 2 – CTR-A Manual)

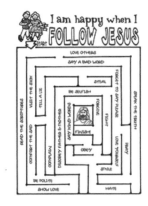

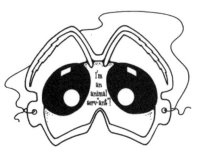

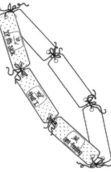

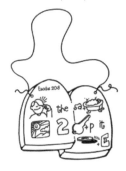

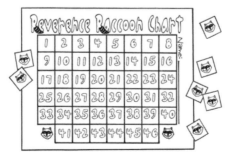

Lesson 1 — Happiness Comes from Choosing the Right

PREPARATION: Review Lesson 1 and the teacher presentation (p. 2) in the *Primary 2—CTR A* manual.

ACTIVITY:
CTR Happiness Wheel

Help children learn that happiness comes from choosing the right. As children spin the wheel, talk about ways they can choose the right and how these choices can help them to be happy.

TO MAKE: Using cardstock paper, copy, color, and cut out the wheel that follows for each child. Attach part A on top of part B with paper fastener (metal or button brad) placed in center. To make a button brad: Sew two buttons together on opposite sides (passing the thread through the same hole) to attach parts A and B.

THOUGHT TREAT (when appropriate): CTR Cookies. Decorate sugar cookie with frosting and write CTR on the cookie with contrasting colored frosting (place frosting in a plastic bag then cut a hole across one corner to squeeze frosting through).

Lesson 2 — Making Right Choices

PREPARATION: Review Lesson 2 and the enrichment activity (p. 9) in the *Primary 2—CTR A* manual.

ACTIVITY:
Choose and Match Puzzle

Help children match cards to the center card that reads, "Think: What would Jesus want me to do?"

TO MAKE: Copy, color, and cut out the puzzle that follows for each child. Place puzzle pieces in a plastic zip-close bag for each child to take home.

THOUGHT TREAT (when appropriate): Think Cookies. Decorate sugar cookies with frosting. Write or draw, using frosting in a tube, something they can do to follow Jesus. Then have children think of what their cookie says, sharing with others ways to follow Jesus.

Part A

Part A

Part B

Lesson 3 — We Are All Heavenly Father's Children

PREPARATION: Review Lesson 3 and discussion #1 (p. 12) in the *Primary 2—CTR A* manual.

ACTIVITY:
Heavenly Family Photo

Help children put themselves in a portrait with Heavenly Father and Jesus and other children to know they are part of a heavenly family. Tell them that we are all Heavenly Father's children, and that we are all brothers and sisters.

TO MAKE: Using cardstock paper, copy, color, and cut out a heavenly family photo and frame that follows for each child. Cut out three 1/4" squares of egg carton for each photo and glue on silhouette squares. Glue a girl or boy on silhouette image on each photo (over the egg carton squares so image will stand out). Fold frame according to directions and glue corners. Tape a string to the back of the framed photo so they can hang it on the wall.

THOUGHT TREAT (when appropriate): Gingerbread Girl or Boy Cookie. Remind children that they are created in the image of Heavenly Father and Jesus.

Lesson 4 — Choose to Follow Jesus

PREPARATION: Review Lesson 4 and scripture story (p. 17-18) in the *Primary 2—CTR A* manual.

ACTIVITY:
Premortal Life Puppet Show

Children can move puppets across the premortal life scene to show that we knew Jesus and Heavenly Father in the spirit world. We had a choice to follow Satan or to follow Jesus. We liked Heavenly Father's plan of happiness and chose to follow Jesus, who followed God's plan. For this reason we were sent to earth to receive a body like Jesus and Heavenly Father and to learn to live Heavenly Father's commandments, like Jesus did. This way we can find happiness and live with Heavenly Father and Jesus again someday.

TO MAKE: Copy, color, and cut out the puppets and scene that follows. Mount puppets on wooden sticks or straws.

THOUGHT TREAT (when appropriate): SMART Snacks. Share apple slices, carrot and celery sticks, and raisins. Remind children that since we were SMART enough to choose to come to earth and receive a body, we need to be SMART enough to eat our fruits and vegetables and other good food to keep our bodies healthy and strong.

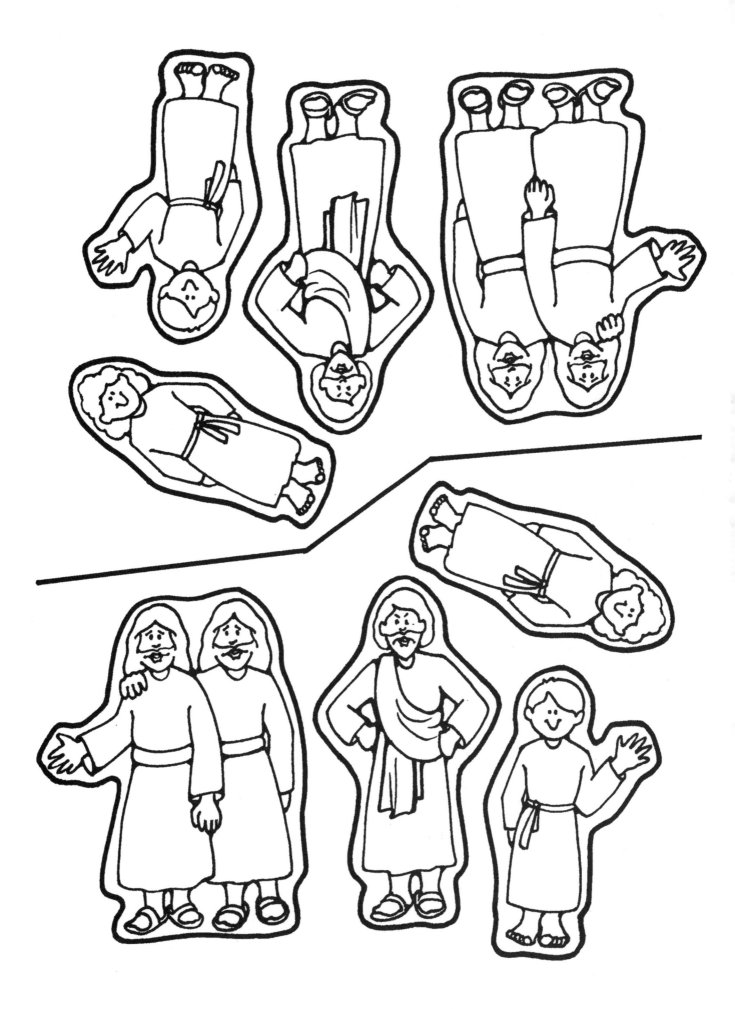

Lesson 5 — Heavenly Father Gave Me Choices

PREPARATION: Review Lesson 5 and summary (p. 23) in the *Primary 2—CTR A* manual.

ACTIVITY:
Choose the Right Slap Game

Help children make righteous choices. As you read the choices below, children can take turns slapping the frown with their left hand if the choice is wrong, or slapping the smile with their right hand if the choice is right. This way they can know to do as Heavenly Father would want them to do—to choose the right.

These situations below apply mostly when children are at church. You can make up other situations they might do at home, e.g., "I clean my room without out being asked."

GOING TO CHURCH CHOICES: • I come to Primary. • I thank my teacher. • I poke my friend instead of folding my arms. • I sing when asked to sing in Primary. • I say, "Excuse me." • I keep my eyes open when the prayer is said. • I bring a friend to Primary. • I yell in the chapel. • I whisper to a friend during the sacrament. • I push a friend away from the fountain. • I walk quietly going to my classroom. • I wait for my turn to have a treat. • I laugh when another child falls down. • I raise my hand in class before talking. • I make noises during class. • I sing with my best voice. • I help the teacher with an activity. • I fold my arms. • I laugh and make fun of someone in class. • I say, "Please" when I need help. • I listen quietly when my teacher tells a story. • I choose the right.

TO MAKE: Copy, color, and cut out the slap pads that follow.

THOUGHT TREAT (when appropriate): Smiling Face Cookies. Decorate cookies with frosting smiles.

Lesson 6 — Families Are Special

PREPARATION: Review Lesson 6 and discussion (p. 26) in the *Primary 2—CTR A* manual.

ACTIVITY:
Missing Family Puzzle

This puzzle includes each family member. Help children know that Heavenly Father planned for us to grow up in families to love and help us. Think of each family member and how SPECIAL they are. Put the puzzle together. Then, take one puzzle piece away and ask, "How would you miss this person if they were not there?" Put the puzzle piece back and have the child tell why this person is special to them. Talk about how we can help each family member feel SPECIAL.

TO MAKE: Using cardstock paper, copy, color, and cut out the puzzle that follows for each child.

THOUGHT TREAT (when appropriate): Happy Family Pancake Faces. Talk about how happy we are when our family is together. Reserve some pancake batter to color some blue for eyes and pink for lips. Fry pancake on one side. After turning, add batter to create face; then turn over to fry, sealing the eyes and lips to the pancake.

| Lesson 7 | Birth of Jesus Brings Joy to the World |

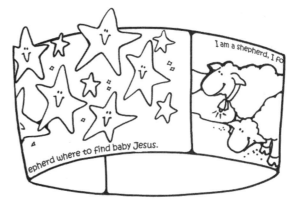

PREPARATION: Review Lesson 7 and scripture story and dramatizations (p. 31-32) in the *Primary 2—CTR A* manual.

ACTIVITY:
Shepherd/Angel Headband

Children can wear the headband to play two roles:
1. *Shepherds:* With the sheep side of the headband facing forward, children can roleplay the shepherds that were looking for Jesus. Say: "I am a shepherd. I found the baby Jesus."
2. *Angels:* Turn the headband with the stars facing forward and pretend to point the way to Jesus, saying: "I am an angel. I told the shepherds where to find the baby Jesus." Tell children the shepherds were led by a bright new star in the sky because they knew it would lead them to the baby Jesus.

TO MAKE: Copy, color, and cut out the headband that follows for each child. Glue or tape the headband together.

THOUGHT TREAT (when appropriate): Baby Jesus' Birthday Cake. Serve a real birthday cake and sing a happy birthday song, adding the name "Jesus" as you sing. Pretend to blow out the unlit candles if at the church, or light them if at home.

| Lesson 8 | Heavenly Father Protects Me |

PREPARATION: Review Lesson 8 and discussion (p. 36) and Enrichment activity #1 (p. 38) in the *Primary 2—CTR A* manual.

ACTIVITY:
Me and Heavenly Father Medallion

Children can wear medallion to strengthen their faith that Heavenly Father will watch over them, bless them, and help them in time of need.

TO MAKE: Using cardstock paper, copy, color, and cut out the medallion that follows for each child. Punch a hole at the top with a paper punch. Lace a 26" piece of yarn or ribbon through the hole and tie at the top. Place around child's neck.

THOUGHT TREAT (when appropriate): Sunshine Sugar Cookies. Decorate round sugar cookies with a frosted sun, making a smiling face and sunrays. Tell children that Heavenly Father is your Sunny Day and Rainy Day Friend. He wants to hear about both your happy times and your sad times.

I am an angel. I told the shepherds where to find baby Jesus.

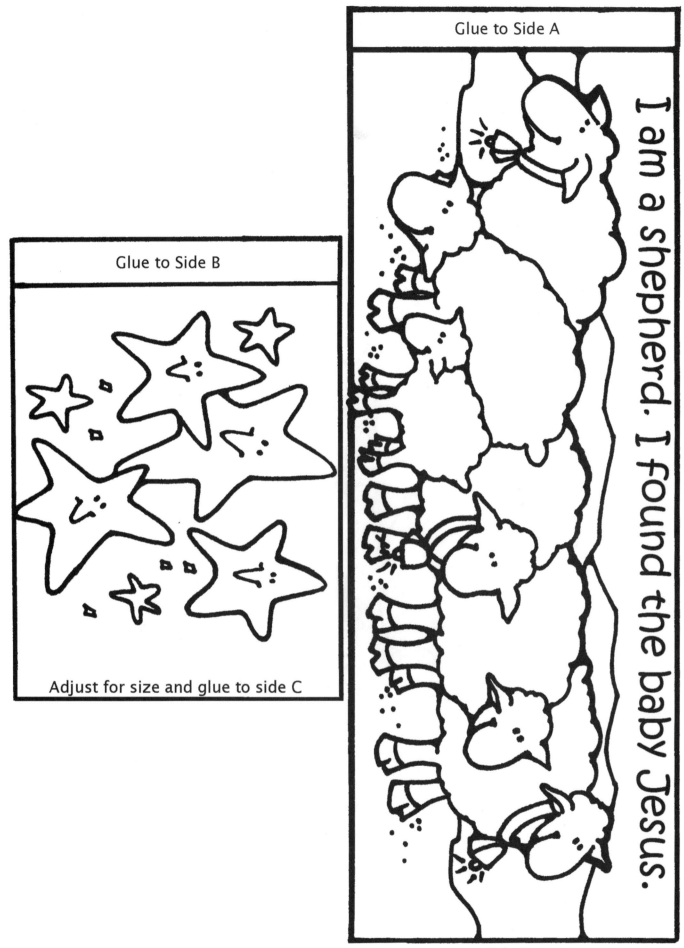

Glue to Side A

Glue to Side B

Adjust for size and glue to side C

I am a shepherd. I found the baby Jesus.

Side B

Lesson 9   I Can Be Like Jesus

PREPARATION: Review Lesson 9 and the scripture story (p. 41) and enrichment activity #2 (p. 43) in the *Primary 2—CTR A* manual.

ACTIVITY:
Scripture Scroll — Luke 2:52

Create a scroll to help children learn how they can be perfect like Jesus. They can roll out this scripture scroll to learn how He became perfect: "Jesus increased in wisdom and stature, and in favour with God and man" (Luke 2:52). Tell children, "We too can be like Jesus."

Discussion: Jesus showed us the way to be baptized (Matt. 3:13-17); He showed love for others (Mark 10:13-16); He forgave those who hurt Him (Luke 23:34); and He taught us how to pray (Matt. 6:5-13). Talk about the scroll, telling children that in Jesus' day, the leaders had scrolls, and many important messages were written on these scrolls.

TO MAKE: Using lightweight paper, copy, color, and cut out the scripture scroll that follows for each child. Glue a wooden craft stick to each side ahead of time, to allow glue to dry. Roll scroll around stick, rolling both ends to the middle with the scripture message inside.

THOUGHT TREAT (when appropriate): Graham Crackers. Serve each child one graham cracker with four sections and talk about the four ways Jesus grew.

Lesson 10   Growing Closer to Heavenly Father

PREPARATION: Review Lesson 10 and the testimony (p. 48) in the *Primary 2—CTR A* manual.

ACTIVITY:
Prayer Rock

Place a rock in a sack with the prayer reminder note. Review the note with children and ask them to place the rock under their pillow at night. When it hits their head they will be reminded to say their prayers. Remind children to pray morning and night and role-play how to pray.

TO MAKE: Copy, color, and cut out the prayer rock label that follows for each child. Place reminder in zip-close plastic bag with a good-size rock.

THOUGHT TREAT (when appropriate): Heart-Shaped Sugar Cookies. Remind children that Heavenly Father will give them warm, peaceful feelings in their heart when they pray.

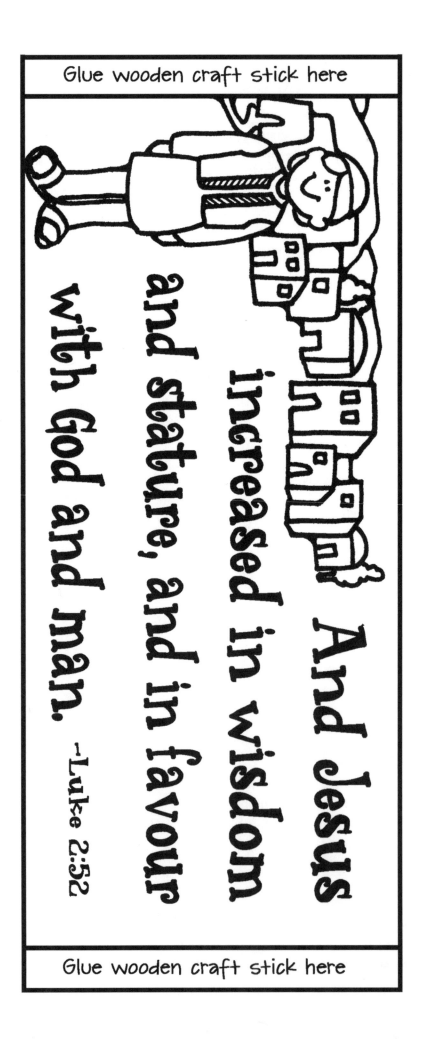

And Jesus increased in wisdom and stature, and in favour with God and man. -Luke 2:52

PRAYER ROCK

To help you remember to say your prayers, place this rock under your pillow.

If you get quickly in your bed
and feel this rock hit your head,
Kneel down and fold your arms to pray,
and thank Heavenly Father for your day.
Ask Him for help in all you do
and know He has great love for you!

PRAYER ROCK

To help you remember to say your prayers, place this rock under your pillow.

If you get quickly in your bed
and feel this rock hit your head,
Kneel down and fold your arms to pray,
and thank Heavenly Father for your day.
Ask Him for help in all you do
and know He has great love for you!

Lesson 11 — Tell Others about Jesus

PREPARATION: Review Lesson 11 and the scripture story and discussion (p. 51) in the *Primary 2—CTR A* manual.

ACTIVITY:
Ammon the Missionary "Script"ure Scene

Help children act out the story or script found in the "script"ure Alma 17:17-25, using the triangle mini-scenes to show how Ammon was a missionary. Begin by saying Ammon was a great servant and a great missionary. Talk about how we can be a missionary today by serving others.

TO MAKE: Using cardstock paper, copy, color, and cut out the scene that follows for each child. Fold and glue where indicated.

THOUGHT TREAT (when appropriate): Tracting Trail Mix. Healthy fruits, cereal, seeds, and nuts make a quick snack for Ammon as he tends King Lamoni's sheep or for today's missionary tracting door to door. As you eat, talk about ways you could tell others about Jesus Christ.

Lesson 12 — I'm Trying to Be Like Jesus

I want to be baptized!

PREPARATION: Review Lesson 12 and enrichment activity #5 (p. 59) in the *Primary 2—CTR A* manual.

ACTIVITY:
Two-sided Baptism Puzzle

Have children put this puzzle together to remind them to follow Jesus and be baptized. On one side of the puzzle is John baptizing Jesus; on the other side is a child being baptized.

TO MAKE: Using cardstock, copy, color, and cut out the puzzle that follows for each child. Cut around outside edge of puzzle first (don't cut puzzle pieces yet). Fold pictures in half on dividing line back-to-back. Glue pictures together (spreading glue over the entire piece, not just the edges). Cut puzzle shapes out as shown on one side (six pieces). Place puzzle in an envelope or plastic bag for each child to take home.

THOUGHT TREAT (when appropriate): Footprint Cookies. Roll sugar cookie dough into two-inch balls. Make imprint in dough with side of fist (to shape foot). Then press down with fingers at the top to make toes or press in chocolate chip or jelly bean toes. Bake.

Fold and glue.

Fold and glue.

Ammon

King Lamoni's Flocks

Lesson 13 — The Gift I Receive After Baptism

PREPARATION: Review Lesson 13 and teacher presentation (p. 62) in the *Primary 2—CTR A* manual.

ACTIVITY:
Holy Ghost Stand-up Card

Help children realize that after they are baptized into The Church of Jesus Christ of Latter-day Saints, they can receive this special gift to help them. Stand-up card reads: "The Holy Ghost speaks to my heart and to my mind."

TO MAKE: Using cardstock, copy, color, and cut out the Holy Ghost card that follows for each child. Before activity, cut dotted lines with an X-ACTO knife or razor blade. Fold where indicated and stand card.

THOUGHT TREAT (when appropriate): Heart-Shaped Treats. Use cookies with heart shaped candies on top or use heart shaped candies. Talk about how the Holy Ghost can speak to our mind and heart.

Lesson 14 — Dare to Choose the Right

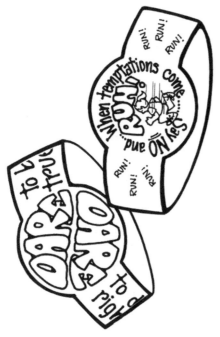

PREPARATION: Review Lesson 14 and the teacher presentation (p. 72) in the *Primary 2—CTR A* manual.

ACTIVITY:
CTR Wristbands

As children wear this wristband, they can be reminded to resist or RUN away from temptation and DARE to do what is right. They will want to be true to gospel teachings as you challenge them to "DARE to do right," and "DARE to be true." As children are reminded that Heavenly Father wants them to return to Him, they will desire to keep His commandments.

TO MAKE: Using cardstock, copy, color, and cut out the wristbands that follow for each child. Attach sticky-back Velcro or a paperclip to bands to make it easy to put on and take off.

THOUGHT TREAT (when appropriate): CTR Treasure Cupcakes. Before baking cupcakes, write "Dare to CTR" on slips of paper, wrap in foil, and drop into cupcake liner as you fill with batter. Surprise! Children find the treasured note baked inside.

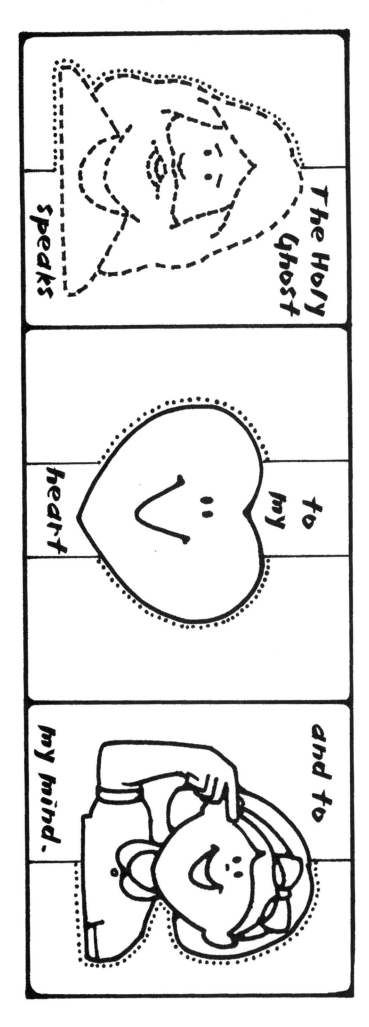
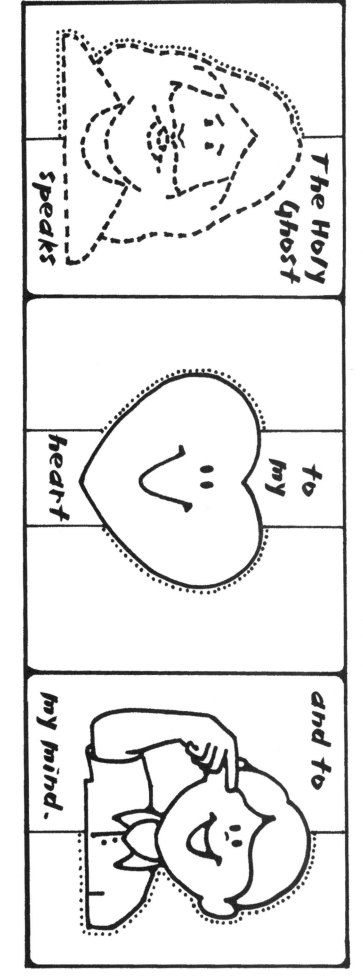

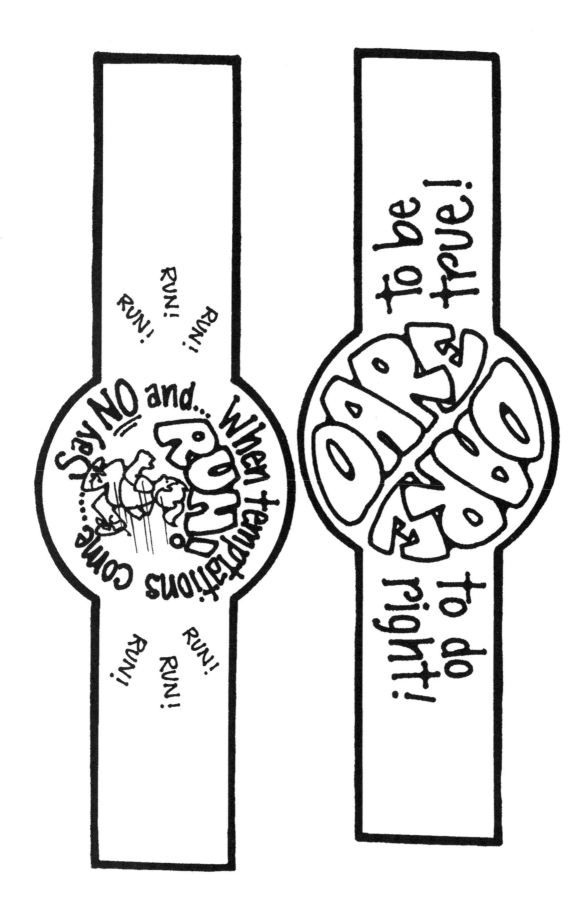

| Lesson 15 | Choose the Right and Follow Jesus |

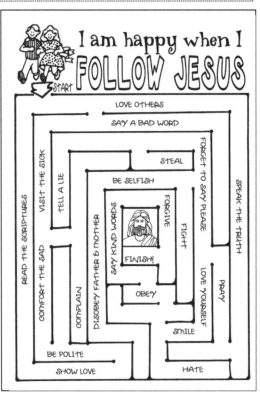

PREPARATION: Review Lesson 15 and testimony (p. 79) in the *Primary 2—CTR A* manual.

ACTIVITY:
Decision Maze

Help children learn how to choose the right and follow Jesus, guiding them through the maze. START at the beginning and guide them past the wrong choices. Pencil or color in the right choices to the FINISH line, where they will find Jesus.

TO MAKE: Copy, color, and cut out the decision maze that follows for each child.

THOUGHT TREAT (when appropriate): Soft Step Marshmallow Feet. Use toothpicks in two large marshmallows to attach five mini marshmallow toes. Use flat (safe) toothpicks or collect sharp toothpicks for safe disposal.

| Lesson 16 | the Priesthood Heals |

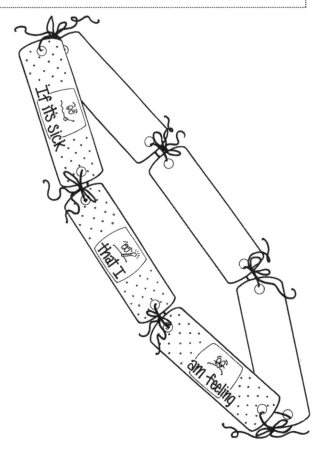

PREPARATION: Review Lesson 16 and testimony (p. 84) in the *Primary 2—CTR A* manual.

ACTIVITY:
Band-aid Bandelo

Children can wear this huge bandelo that reads: "If it's sick that I am feeling, I'll let the priesthood do the healing." Tell children that Jesus Christ has the power to heal and has given the priesthood to us to help heal the sick. Place a band-aid bandelo around each child's shoulder to cross over the chest.

TO MAKE: Using cardstock, copy, color, and cut out the band-aid bandelo that follows for each child. Punch holes at each end. Tie yarn or ribbon to connect ends.

THOUGHT TREAT (when appropriate): Bandage-shaped Wafer Cookie. Decorate a frosted smile in the center of each wafer cookie.

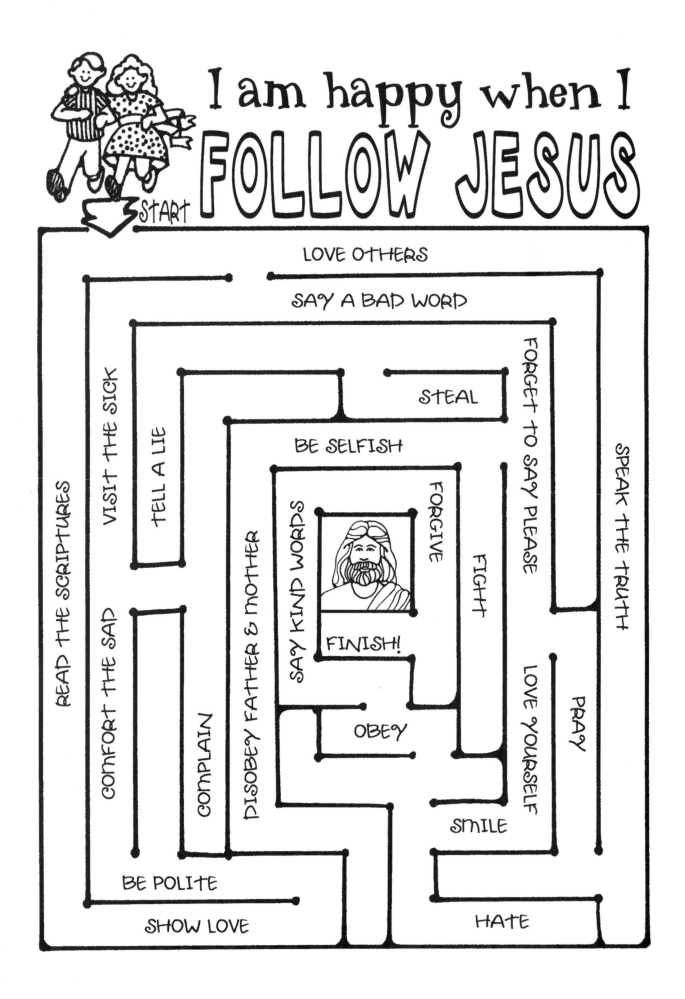

1. If it's sick

2. that I

3. am feeling

4. I'll let

5. the priesthood

6. do the healing

Lesson 17	The Priesthood Can Help Me

PREPARATION: Review Lesson 17 and scripture story (p. 86) in the *Primary 2—CTR A* manual.

ACTIVITY:
Calming the Seas Moving Ship Scene

Use the moving ship scene to talk about and remind children of the story in Mark 4:39 where Jesus calmed the storm. Tell children that Jesus helps and blesses us through the power of the priesthood. Hold onto the handle on the back of the scene with one hand and with the other, use the stick to move the boat back and forth. To simulate a rough sea, move the handle fast; to show a calm sea, move the handle slow.

TO MAKE: Copy, color, and cut out the ship scene, boat, and handle that follows. Glue or tape the top half of a wooden craft stick to the back of the boat. Cut a slit in the scene where indicated (in the water). Place the boat in the scene by inserting the stick into the slit, allowing you to rock the boat back and forth. Fan-fold the handle (shown on the pattern page) and glue or tape the handle to the back of the scene just above the slit.

THOUGHT TREAT (when appropriate): Banana Boat with Cheese Sails. Cut a banana in half crosswise and lengthwise and insert a slice of cheese with a toothpick for the sail. As you eat, talk about the story from Mark 4:35–41, showing the ship scene (above).

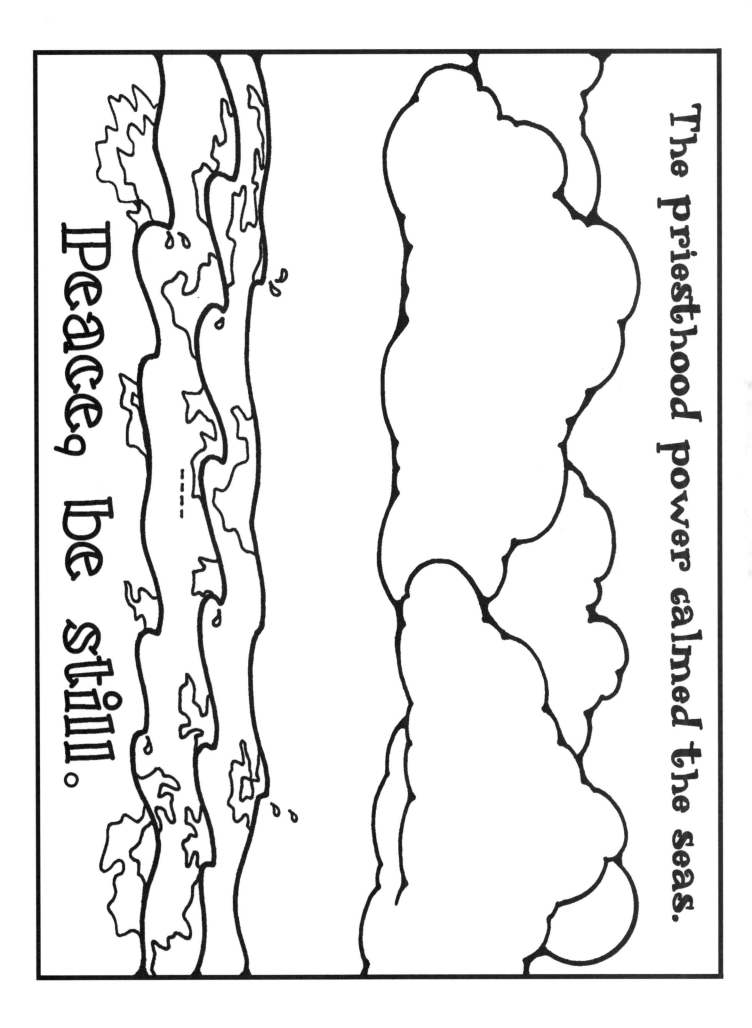

The priesthood power calmed the seas.

Peace, be still.

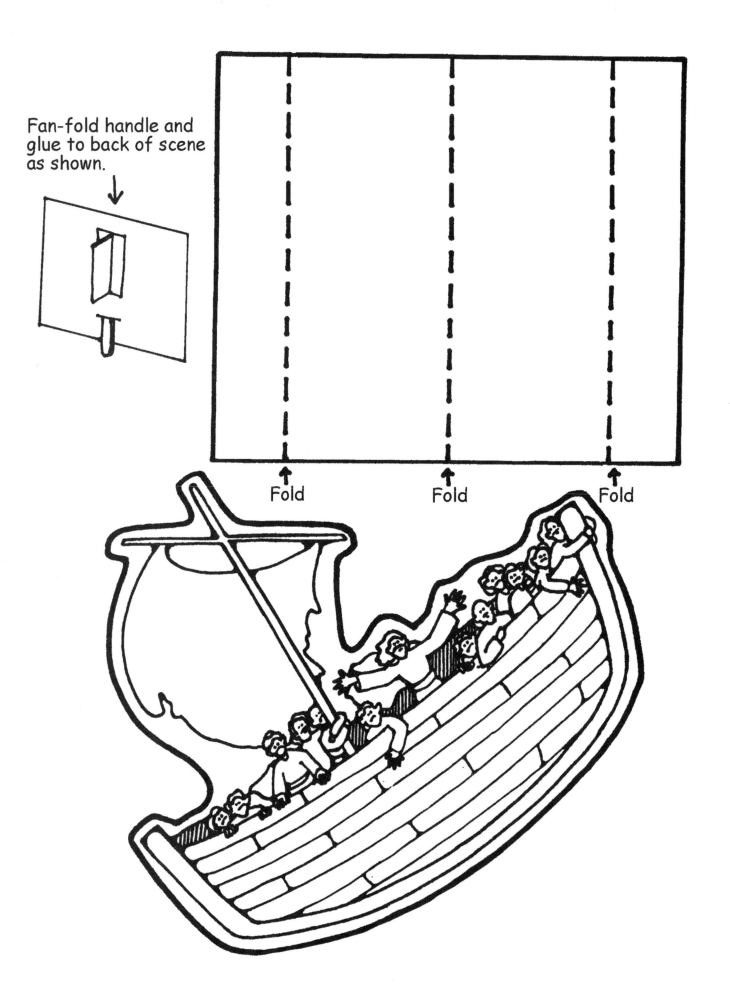

Fan-fold handle and glue to back of scene as shown.

Fold   Fold   Fold

Lesson 18	Heavenly Father Answers My Prayers

PREPARATION: Review Lesson 18 and enrichment activity #1 (p. 94) in the *Primary 2—CTR A* manual.

ACTIVITY:
"YES" and "NO" Wristbands

Children can wear "YES" and "NO" wristbands to help them make decisions that are best. This will help them judge how Heavenly Father might answer their prayer. The "YES" wristband reads: "YES, because it's OK." The "NO" wristband reads: "NO, because it is best for me."

Situations to Discuss: The lesson suggests several parent-child situations where children pretend to be the parent. They decide what is best for the children. This way they can learn to make decisions like Heavenly Father does for us as His children when He answers our prayers.

Here are a few situations where children pretend to be the parent. They decide what is best for their children.

1. Your child wants his dinner, but the dog is hungry too. Do you feed your child dinner first? "NO." Why do you say that?

2. Your child wants to run out on the icy, slippery porch. Do you let him? "NO." Why do you say that?

3. The work is done, and it's time for fun. Do you go to the park? "YES." Why do you say that?

4. Your child needs his sleep, and it's time to go to bed. He still wants to play. "NO." Why do you say that?

5. The fish tank is dirty. Do you let your fish swim in dirty water? "NO." Why do you say that?

6. Aunt Susan is sick and needs some loving care. Do you leave her bedside? "NO." Why do you say that?

7. Your child's favorite TV show is on, and he has helped you set the table for dinner. Do you let him watch TV? "YES." Why do you say that?

To Make: Copy, color, and cut out a "YES" and a "NO" wristband that follows for each child. Attach wristbands with sticky-back Velcro or tape.

THOUGHT TREAT (when appropriate): "YES" and "NO" Cookies. Give children a cookie with a "Y" on it and a cookie with an "N" on it.

Lesson 19	*Jesus Loves Me*

PREPARATION: Review Lesson 19 and the two scripture stories (p. 97) in the *Primary 2—CTR A* manual.

ACTIVITY:
Mirror Message Poster

Help children create a poster that frames a child's face they can post on their mirror. As they look at the poster on the mirror, they peer through the cutout heart into the mirror to see themselves reflected there. As they read the loving words, "Jesus loves me!" they will truly feel His love. Tell children, "As you get to know your Savior Jesus Christ, you will know what He has done for you and how much He loves you."

TO MAKE: Using cardstock, copy, color, and cut out the poster that follows for each child (cutting out the heart inside the poster so the child's image can be seen through the heart).

THOUGHT TREAT (when appropriate): Heart Cut-out Sandwich or Heart Miniature Sandwiches. Make a sandwich and cut the center out to resemble the poster, or let children eat the miniature cut-out heart sandwich.

Lesson 20	I Want to Learn About Jesus

PREPARATION: Review Lesson 20 and treasure hunt activity (p. 103) in the *Primary 2—CTR A* manual.

ACTIVITY:
Scripture Bookmark

Children can place this bookmark in their scriptures to remind them that the teachings of Jesus are a great treasure! Each time they read the scriptures it's like going on a treasure hunt. D&C 89:19 tells us that we will find "great treasures of knowledge, even hidden treasures," many of which are in the scriptures. Help children look up and read John 13:17 (happy are they if they know the scriptures).

TO MAKE: Using cardstock, copy, color, and cut out the scripture bookmark that follows for each child. Punch holes around the border. Weave yarn through holes and tie a bow at the top.

THOUGHT TREAT (when appropriate): Scripture Wafers. Select four wafer-type cookies in the shape of scriptures. As you eat each cracker, name the standard works: Bible, Book of Mormon, Pearl of Great Price, and Doctrine and Covenants.

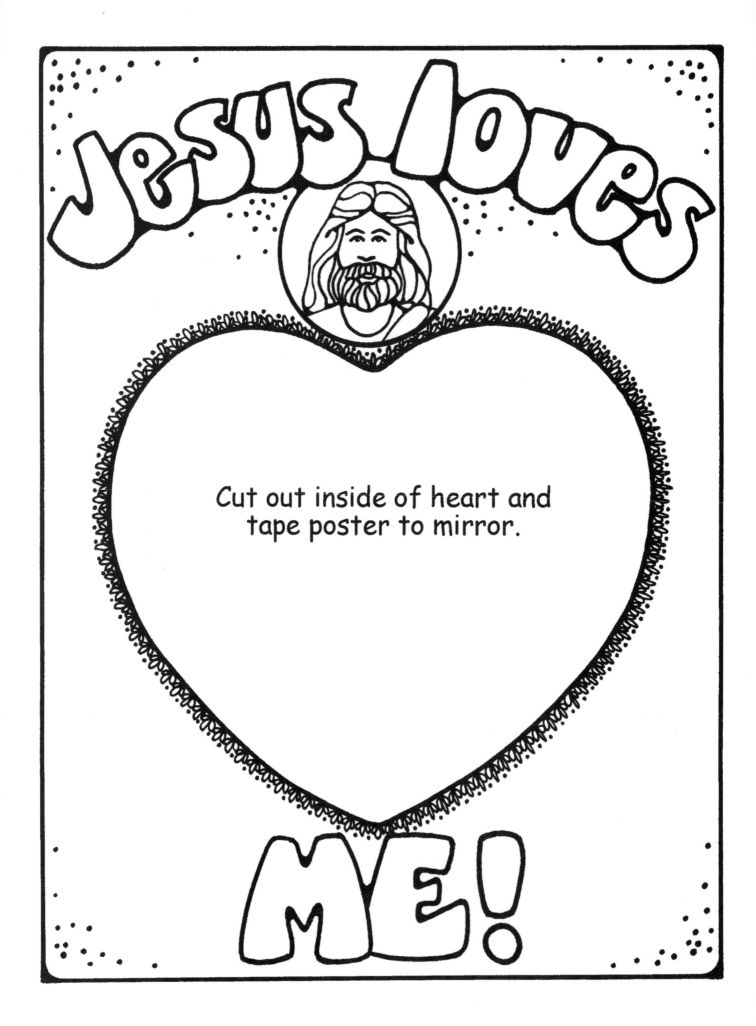

The
teachings
of Jesus
are a
great
treasure!

The
teachings
of Jesus
are a
great
treasure!

The
teachings
of Jesus
are a
great
treasure!

Lesson 21	Reverence Begins with Me

PREPARATION: Review Lesson 21 and enrichment activity #3 (p. 112) in the *Primary 2—CTR A* manual.

ACTIVITY:
Reverence Raccoon Cap & Storybook

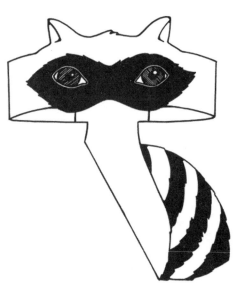

1. Children can wear this Reverence Raccoon cap as you talk about the importance of reverence and role-play reverent actions, e.g., folding arms for prayer, closing eyes, bowing head, and listening while the prayer is said.
2. The Reverence Raccoon Storybook shows ways to be reverent and happy at home and church. Children can act out the reverence actions in story.
3. Talk about Nephite children, how they showed reverence when around Jesus (3 Nephi 17:11-12, 21-24).
4. Use the **Reverence Raccoon Chart** (shown below, detailed in the Introduction).

TO MAKE: Using cardstock, copy, color, and cut out the cap and storybook that follows for each child. To make cap, glue or tape sides together, matching parts A–C. Attach tail back to parts C and D. To make storybook, staple pages together.

THOUGHT TREAT (when appropriate): Raccoon "Eye" Love You Sugar Cookies. Frost round cookies with white frosting and place a black gumdrop in the center—serve two cookies each to complete the raccoon eyes. Talk about raccoons, how they are so eager to be clean, that they wash their food before they eat it. Say, "I'll bet they even fold their arms and bow their head when a prayer is said." Reverence Raccoon says, "Reverence Begins with Me!"

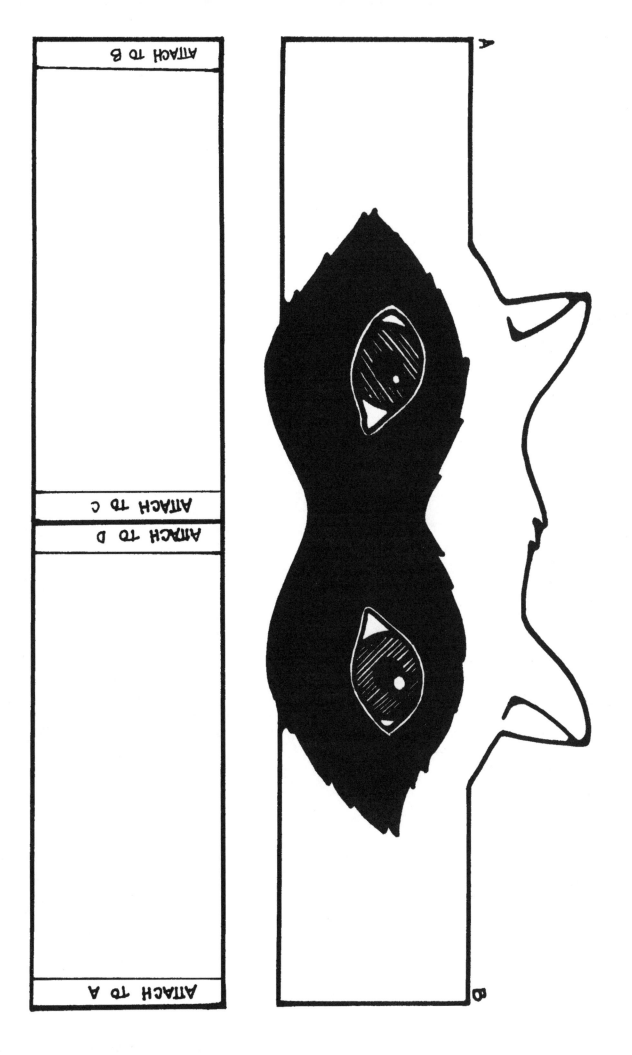

Lesson 22   *Shine Brightly*

PREPARATION: Review Lesson 22 and testimony (p. 117) in the *Primary 2—CTR A* manual.

ACTIVITY:
Peacemaker Light Switch Cover

Children can place this cover over their bedroom light switch to remind them to shine brightly each day, showing love and concern for others. Remind them they can make their home more peaceful by doing kind deeds and helping those in need.

TO MAKE: Using cardstock, copy, color, and cut out the light switch cover that follows for each child. Ahead of time, cut out center of light switch cover with scissors or a Xacto knife or razor blade.

THOUGHT TREAT (when appropriate): Peaceful Pudding. Serve a large bowl or individual cups of pudding with a whipped cream smile on top to remind children that when we are a peacemaker we are happy and others are happy too. Talk of ways they can be a peacemaker, such as sharing toys, waiting for their turn at the drinking fountain, and raising their hand before they speak in class.

Lesson 23   *Jesus Is the Good Shepherd*

PREPARATION: Review Lesson 23, and scripture story and testimony summary (p. 121) in the *Primary 2—CTR A* manual.

ACTIVITY:
Find the Lost Lamb Hidden Picture Poster

Tell children about Jesus as the good shepherd who found the lost lamb. Have children pretend to be a good shepherd and find the lost lamb . . . wearing tennis shoes, a necktie, baseball hat, bell, bow tie, and more. Tell children, "Color the lost lambs as soon as you 'ewe' find them."

TO MAKE: Copy, color, and cut out the picture poster for each child.

THOUGHT TREAT (when appropriate): Lambs in the Corral. Make a corral or fence out of graham cracker sections, gluing the corral/fence together with frosting. The corral holds in the little lambs that may run away and get lost. Enclose lambs (miniature white marshmallows) inside the graham cracker corral.

I'm a
PEACEMAKER!

Shine Brightly!

I Can

Cut
Out

I'm a
PEACEMAKER!

Shine Brightly!

I Can

Cut
Out

Find the Little

LOST LAMB

Find the little lost lamb...
- wearing tennis shoes
- wearing a necktie
- with a big smile

- wearing a baseball hat
- wearing a bell
- with polka-dots
- that is black

- wearing a bowtie
- wearing earrings
- wearing shorts
- wearing a belt

- holding a flower
- wearing glasses
- without ears
- wearing a bow

Lesson 24   Give Thanks

PREPARATION: Review Lesson 24 and enrichment activity # 1 (p. 127) in the *Primary 2—CTR A* manual.

ACTIVITY:
Gratitude Gopher's Grab Bag

Ways to use the Grab Bag:

1. Children can reach into bag before they pray to find things to tell Heavenly Father they are thankful for.

2. *Play the Gratitude Gopher Game:* Divide into teams and have children take turns drawing a card from the bag. If they draw a Gratitude Gopher card, they tell what they are thankful for. If they draw a gratitude card, they can tell why they are thankful for the item on the card. **TO WIN:** Gratitude Gopher cards are worth five points and gratitude cards are worth one point. The team with the most points wins!

TO MAKE: Copy, color, and cut out the grab bag visuals that follow for each child. Glue the grab bag label on small paper lunch sack or slip inside a zip-close plastic bag. Place squares inside.

THOUGHT TREAT (when appropriate): Gopher Graham Crackers. Draw a gopher on a graham cracker using chocolate frosting from a tube, adding teeth (white frosting or miniature marshmallows). Tell children that when they show gratitude, like Grateful Gopher, they feel happy (point at Gratitude Gopher's big, toothy smile).

Lesson 25   Saying Thank-you

PREPARATION: Review Lesson 25 and art activity (p. 131) in the *Primary 2—CTR A* manual.

ACTIVITY:
Courtesy Thank-you Card

Help children learn to say thank-you with this little note of appreciation. They can give this courtesy thank-you card to someone who has helped them in church, the neighborhood, or at home. The card could be sent to mom or dad, bishop, chorister, special teacher, or friend.

TO MAKE: Using cardstock, copy, color, and cut out the courtesy thank-you card that follows for each child. Fan-fold and glue front flap to middle. Children can sign and deliver card.

THOUGHT TREAT (when appropriate): Thankful Foods. Provide finger foods children are thankful for, such as tiny crackers, raisins, marshmallows, or carrot or apple slices. Before they eat, they can say "thank you" for every item.

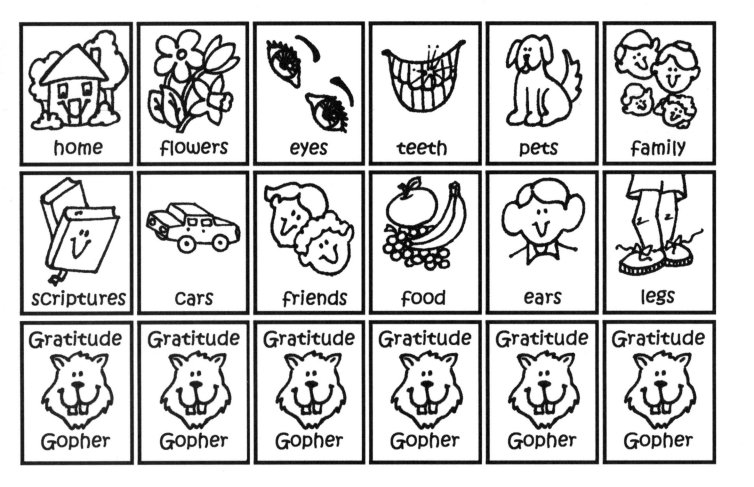

home	flowers	eyes	teeth	pets	family
scriptures	cars	friends	food	ears	legs
Gratitude Gopher	Gratitude Gopher	Gratitude Gopher	Gratitude Gopher	Gratitude Gopher	Gratitude Gopher

GRATITUDE GOPHER GRAB BAG

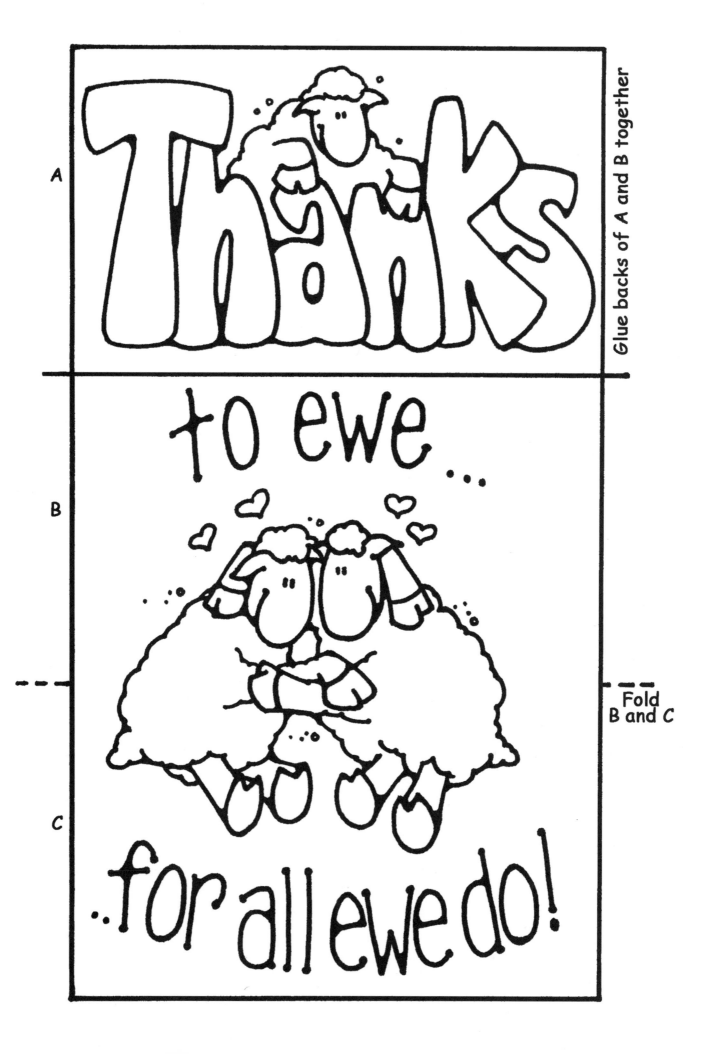

Thanks
to ewe...
...for all ewe do!

Glue backs of A and B together

Fold B and C

Lesson 26 — Choosing the Right Brings Happy Feelings

PREPARATION: Review Lesson 26 and testimony (p. 137) in the *Primary 2—CTR A* manual.

ACTIVITY:
Happy Heart Medallion

Talk to children about the medallion that reminds them that "Choosing the right brings happy feelings."

TO MAKE: Using cardstock, copy, color, and cut out the happy heart medallion parts that follow for each child. Fold arms in half and glue back to back*. Fan-fold arms. Glue hands to arms on part B then glue back-to-back. Glue part A arm on the left- and right-inside of hearts with thumbs up. Then glue hearts back-to-back. Tie ends of yarn or ribbon through each hole and place around child's neck. *Note: If you copy pattern on cardstock and the arms are too stiff, only use half the arm, cutting the other half away.

THOUGHT TREAT (when appropriate): Cherry "Cheery Smile" Cookies. Add finely chopped maraschino cherries to sugar cookie dough (with 1/4 cup extra flour). Roll out dough and cut into heart shapes. Bake at 350° for 8-10 minutes. Tell children that this cherry cookie is to remind them to be sure and wear a "cheery" happy smile to show others that you want to choose the right.

Lesson 27 — Happy Times Are Sharing Times

PREPARATION: Review Lesson 27 and activity/summary (p. 141) in the *Primary 2—CTR A* manual.

ACTIVITY:
Share-treats

Wrap up a candy bar and/or stick of gum for the child to share in class or at home. The wrapper(s) invite them to share. Since there are two sticks of gum, children could share one stick in class with a friend and take the other home to share. Talk about the importance of sharing and how they can share.

TO MAKE: Using lightweight paper, copy, color, and cut out the treat wrappers that follow for each child. Tape the treat wrappers around candy bars and/or sticks of chewing gum.

THOUGHT TREAT (when appropriate): Candy bar or chewing gum to share using the wrapper labels shown above, and one extra of each to wrap up and take home to repeat activity.

47

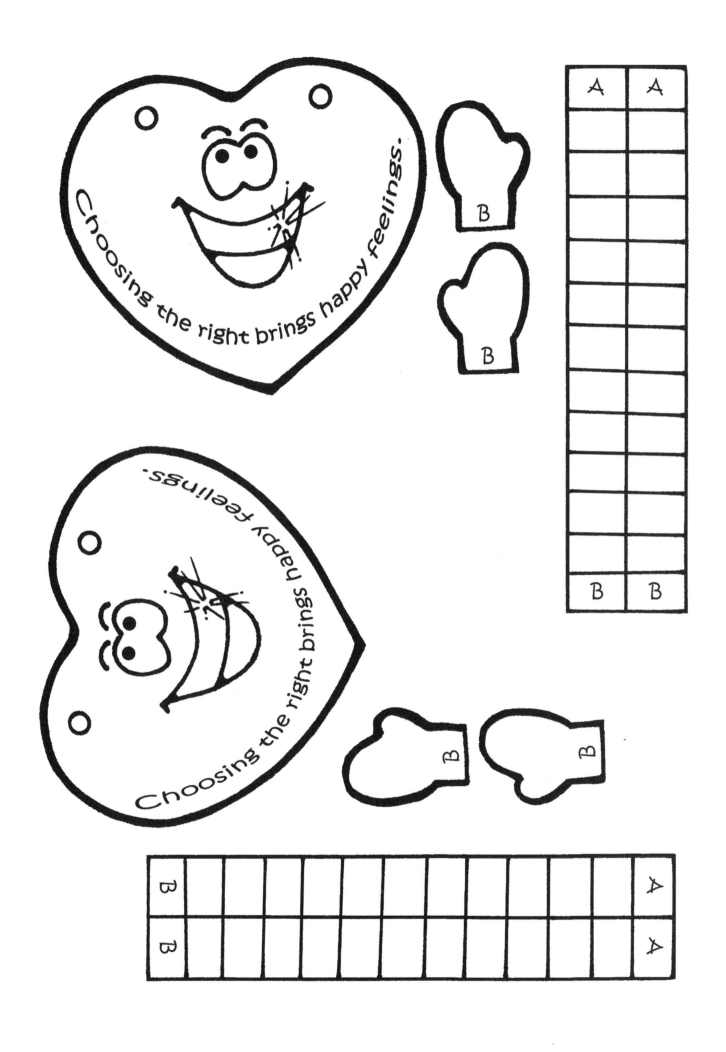

Lesson 28   # Be Kind to Others

Bite-size Memorize

This is m[eye] [commandments] to ye [love] 1 a[n]r as [eye] have [God]+[love] U.

John 15:12

PREPARATION: Review Lesson 28, scripture, and song (p. 145) in the *Primary 2—CTR A* manual.

ACTIVITY:
Bite-size Memorize Poster

Help children memorize John 15:12 using this picture poster. Remind them that Jesus wants us to be kind to others. Talk about how Jesus showed kindness and how they can show kindness to their friends and family.

TO MAKE: Copy, color, and cut out the bite-size memorize poster that follows for each child.

THOUGHT TREAT (when appropriate): Give-Away Goodies. Make a special treat children can give to someone, such as the bishop or neighbor or the elderly, to show kindness.

Lesson 29   # Let My Light Shine

PREPARATION: Review Lesson 29, scripture story, object lesson, and discussion (p. 150) in the *Primary 2—CTR A* manual.

ACTIVITY:
Example Candle Mobile

Use this candle mobile to remind children to let their light shine in CHURCH, at SCHOOL, and at HOME as Jesus did. Jesus was our greatest example (Matt. 5:14-16). As you turn the mobile, discuss how they can be an example in each of these areas.

TO MAKE: Using cardstock, copy, color, and cut out the candle that follows for each child. Fold candle and tape a 16" string halfway down on inside. Glue tabs. Hang mobile.

THOUGHT TREAT (when appropriate): Candle Cake. Place a candle in a cupcake and light it if you are at home, or pretend to light and blow-out the candle if you are at church. Tell children, "When we choose the right we let our light shine. By choosing the right we are good examples to our friends and family at church, school, and at home."

This is my commandment, That ye love one another, as I have loved you.

John 15:12

shine!

SCHOOL

example.

light

HOME

be an

Let your

CHURCH

I can

Fold and glue

shine!

SCHOOL

example.

light

HOME

be an

Let your

CHURCH

I can

Fold and glue

Lesson 30	Follow Jesus and Obey

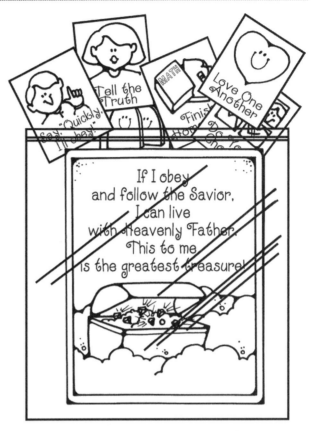

PREPARATION: Review Lesson 30 and enrichment activity (p. 159) in the *Primary 2—CTR A* manual.

ACTIVITY:
Heavenly Treasure Hunt

Have a treasure hunt so children can find a treasure bag filled with treats and obedience reminder cards to remind them to be obedient and follow Jesus. This way they can receive the greatest treasure—to live with Heavenly Father again.

Treasure Hunt:

1. Write clues on the backs of the cards (shown right) and hide them. When children go to find them, have them go from one to the next, reading the cards aloud as they find them, then reading the clues to the next. The last card found should lead them to finding the large treasure card (shown right): "If I obey and follow the Savior, I can live with Heavenly Father. This to me is the greatest treasure!"

2. Talk about what it would be like to obtain this treasure. We would have peace and happiness, we could be with our families forever, everyone would learn about the gospel.

3. *Option:* The clue cards could be placed under objects children could find; for example, the card with the clock, "Come Home on Time," could be placed under a clock, and the clue written on this card could lead them to the books where the clue card "Finish Homework" could be found.

4. *Note:* If children need coaxing to find clues, you might say when they are getting cold, colder, warm, warmer, hot, or freezing.

TO MAKE: Copy, color, and cut out the treasure label and cards that follow for each child. Glue label to the back of a lunch sack or slip inside a zip-close plastic bag for each child to take home. Place treats and obedience reminder cards inside bag.

THOUGHT TREAT (when appropriate): Sweetest Treasure Treats. Place small candies inside the heavenly treasure hunt bag. Remind children that candy is sweet and fun to eat, but it doesn't last long. The sweetest treasure can last forever. That treasure is to live with Heavenly Father again. Read the treasure sack label above to learn the message.

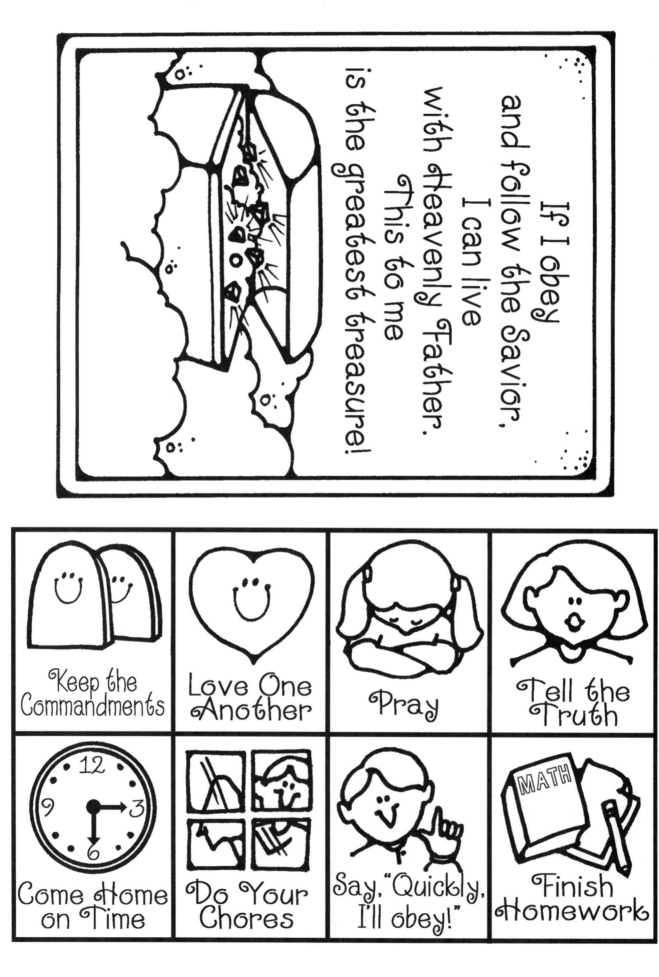

If I obey
and follow the Savior,
I can live
with Heavenly Father.
This to me
is the greatest treasure!

Keep the
Commandments

Love One
Another

Pray

Tell the
Truth

Come Home
on Time

Do Your
Chores

Say, "Quickly,
I'll obey!"

Finish
Homework

Lesson 31	Obeying the Law

PREPARATION: Review Lesson 31, preparation 5 (p. 162), and the child participation and enrichment activity #2 (p. 166) in the *Primary 2—CTR A* manual.

ACTIVITY:
Law Obedience Badge

Have children wear this badge to remind them to respect and obey the laws of the land. Talk about raising their right hand to make a promise. Have children do this as they say, "I promise to obey the laws."

TO MAKE: Using cardstock, copy, color, and cut out the badge that follows for each child. Place a safety pin on the badge to pin to child's clothing.

THOUGHT TREAT (when appropriate): Five Olives on Five Fingers. Ask children to name five rules in their family to keep them safe and happy, such as picking up toys so others don't fall on them, putting away their clothes so they will know where they are, or waiting for their turn at doing something so everyone will have a turn and no one will feel left out.

Lesson 32	Show Love

PREPARATION: Review Lesson 32, attention activity (p. 168) and enrichment activity (p. 171) in the *Primary 2—CTR A* manual.

ACTIVITY:
I Love You Pop-up Card

Encourage each child to give this card to someone they love. Talk to them of other ways they can show their love, by helping others.

TO MAKE: Using cardstock, copy, color, and cut out the Love You pop-up card that follows for each child. Fold down center of heart and cut on dotted line. Fold bottom lines of heart so heart leans out. Fold between A and B. Spread glue on back side of B and glue to A.

THOUGHT TREAT (when appropriate): Heart-to-Heart Biscuit. Make baking powder biscuits by rolling out and cutting out two heart-shaped biscuits for each child, laying half of the heart over the other. When sharing this heart-warming treat, tell children that when they show love to another by helping, they warm two hearts.

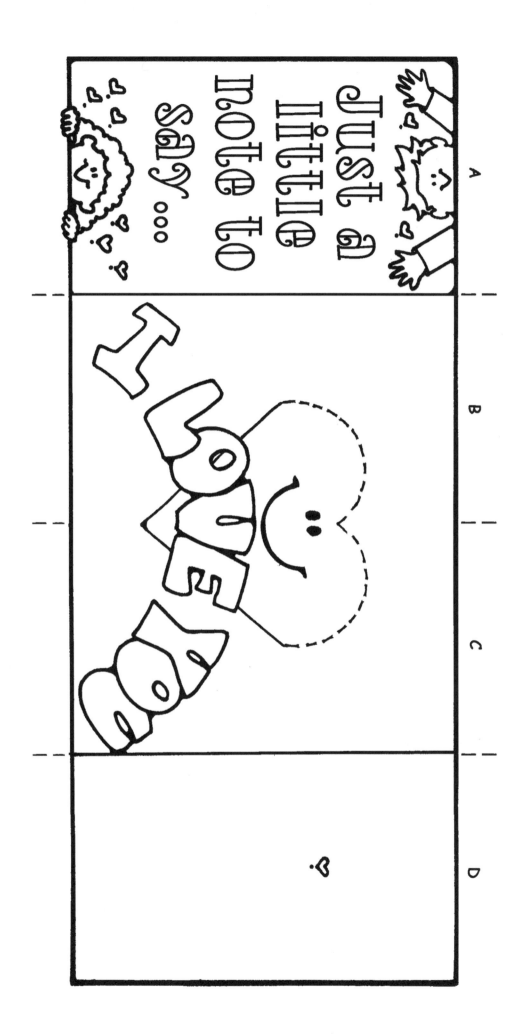

Lesson 33 — Showing Love as I Share

PREPARATION: Review Lesson 33, activity (How We Pay Tithing), and enrichment activity #3 (p. 180) in the *Primary 2—CTR A* manual.

ACTIVITY:
My Tithing Envelope

Create a tithing storage envelope for each child to store ready-to-pay tithing money and receipt forms. Explain that as we pay our tithing, we show love for Heavenly Father and Jesus. Help child fill out a sample tithing envelope, leaving the amount to be filled in later.

TO MAKE: Copy, color, and cut out the My Tithing envelope that follows for each child. Fold edges and glue envelope, leaving top flap free to open and close.

THOUGHT TREAT (when appropriate): Ten Bite-size Cookies. Help children give one away to the bishop, explaining to the bishop of your ward that you are helping the children share 1/10th.

Lesson 34 — Tell the Truth

PREPARATION: Review Lesson 34 and enrichment activity #4 (p. 185) in the *Primary 2—CTR A* manual.

ACTIVITY:
Trevor and Trina Truth Sack Puppets

Sometimes it's not easy to tell the truth, but if children have their very own Trevor or Trina truth sack puppets, they can role-play truth-telling situations. Put on a puppet show, acting out different situations you might encounter with honesty. See if your audience agrees with your solutions to the situation.

TO MAKE: Copy, color, and cut out the Trevor Truth (for boys) or the Trina Truth (for girls) sack puppets that follow for each child. Glue the girl or boy head to bottom of a small lunch sack, and glue the chin up under the flap. When children move the sack flap up and down, the puppet's mouth opens to say, "I can be strong and tell the truth."

THOUGHT TREAT (when appropriate): I "Chews" to Tell the Truth Chewing Gum.

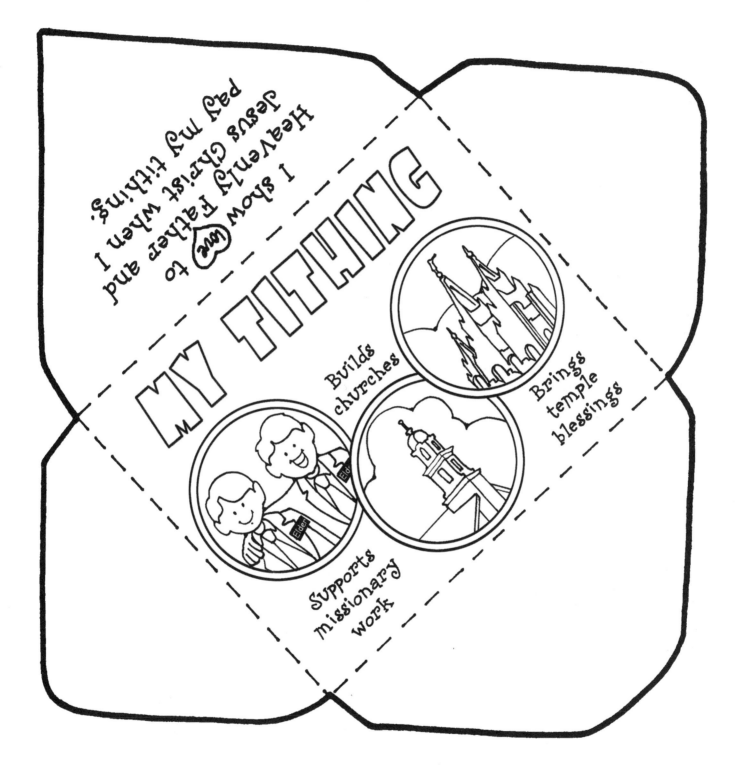

MY TITHING

I show love to Heavenly Father and Jesus Christ when I pay my tithing.

Builds churches

Supports missionary work

Brings temple blessings

Lesson 35	Heavenly Father Gave Me Talents

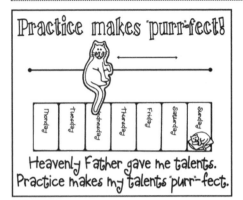

Practice makes 'purr'-fect!

Monday Tuesday Wednesday Thursday Friday Saturday Sunday

Heavenly Father gave me talents.
Practice makes my talents 'purr'-fect.

PREPARATION: Review Lesson 35 and teacher presentation (p. 189) in the *Primary 2—CTR A* manual.

ACTIVITY:
Talent Tally

Tally helps remind children each day of a talent they can practice. Create a Monday-through-Sunday cat walk, moving the cat along on a string each day to remind them that "Practice Makes 'Purr'-fect." Each time they try something, it gets easier and easier. Soon they will purr with delight that they have developed a talent, such as being kind to others, helping at home, learning to read, drawing, painting, creating something, playing an instrument, cleaning up their room, or taking care of their pets.

TO MAKE: Copy, color, and cut out the talent tally that follows for each child. Poke a hole in the left and right side on the "X". Run string through both holes and tie in front so there is no lag in string. Tape cat over knot and show how it moves back and forth, Monday through Sunday.

THOUGHT TREAT (when appropriate): "Purr"-fect Bread. Form bread dough into the shape of a cat and bake at 375° for 10-15 minutes. Thread three black threads through cat's mouth with a needle and clip ends. As children eat the cat-shaped bread, pull out thread (cat's whiskers) one at a time and name three talents they want to "purr"-fect.

Lesson 36	Follow Jesus

WISE MAN
Built his house upon a rock.

PREPARATION: Review Lesson 36, scripture story, discussion, and song (p. 195) in the *Primary 2—CTR A* manual.

ACTIVITY:
Wise Man, Foolish Man Flip-Flag

(1) Sing "The Wise Man and Foolish Man," p. 281 in the Children's Songbook.
(2) Create a wise man and foolish man flag that children can flip back and forth to remind them to follow the prophet. When they have two choices to make, they should slow down and pray (show flag moving slowly). Then when they have made the right decision they can flip quickly to the wise man side. Talk about specific blessings that came to the wise man and that can come to us as we follow the prophet. (3) Give children the cookie recipe and house pattern to take home to make their own cookies.

TO MAKE: Copy, color, and cut out the flag and cookie recipe and pattern that follows for each child. Mount a wooden craft stick in the bottom center, fold, and glue back-to-back.

THOUGHT TREAT (when appropriate): Smiling House Sugar Cookies. Use the cookie recipe that follows and the house pattern to cut out sugar cookie dough. Decorate each house with a smile to remind children of the wise man's house and how choosing the right can put a smile on everyone's face.

House
Cookie
Pattern

Practice makes "purr-fect!

Monday

Tuesday

Wednesday

Thursday

Friday

Saturday

Sunday

Heavenly Father gave me talents.
Practice makes my talents "purr"-fect.
Practice makes "purr"-fect.

Paste to
cat back

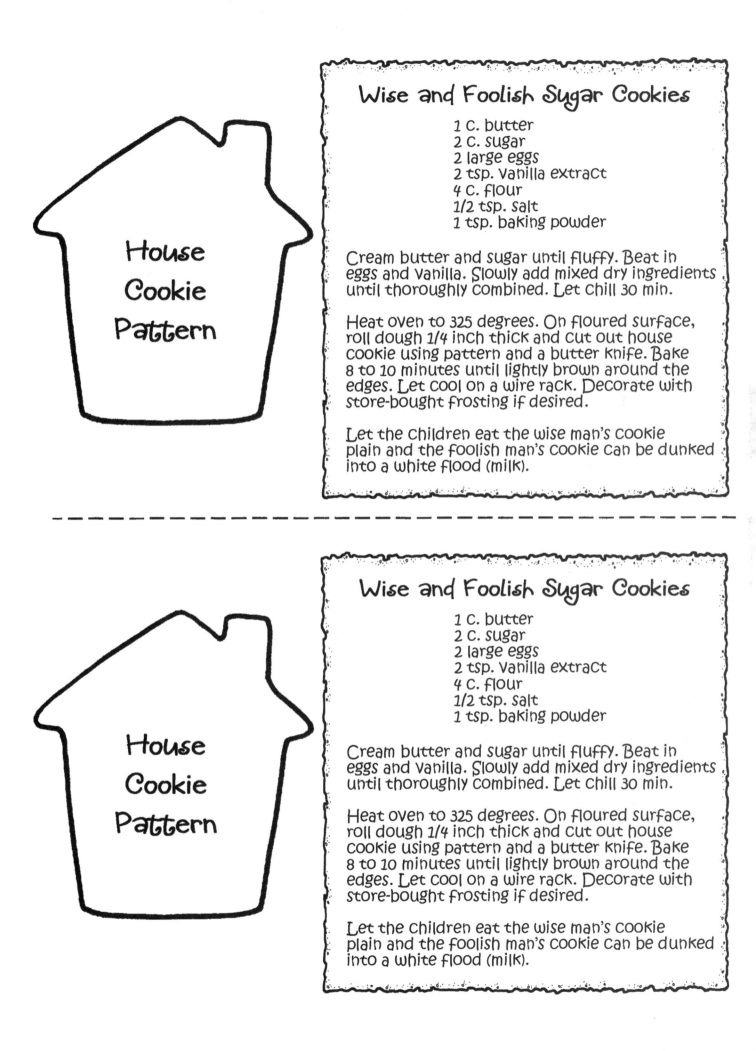

House Cookie Pattern

Wise and Foolish Sugar Cookies

1 C. butter
2 C. sugar
2 large eggs
2 tsp. vanilla extract
4 C. flour
1/2 tsp. salt
1 tsp. baking powder

Cream butter and sugar until fluffy. Beat in eggs and vanilla. Slowly add mixed dry ingredients until thoroughly combined. Let chill 30 min.

Heat oven to 325 degrees. On floured surface, roll dough 1/4 inch thick and cut out house cookie using pattern and a butter knife. Bake 8 to 10 minutes until lightly brown around the edges. Let cool on a wire rack. Decorate with store-bought frosting if desired.

Let the children eat the wise man's cookie plain and the foolish man's cookie can be dunked into a white flood (milk).

House Cookie Pattern

Wise and Foolish Sugar Cookies

1 C. butter
2 C. sugar
2 large eggs
2 tsp. vanilla extract
4 C. flour
1/2 tsp. salt
1 tsp. baking powder

Cream butter and sugar until fluffy. Beat in eggs and vanilla. Slowly add mixed dry ingredients until thoroughly combined. Let chill 30 min.

Heat oven to 325 degrees. On floured surface, roll dough 1/4 inch thick and cut out house cookie using pattern and a butter knife. Bake 8 to 10 minutes until lightly brown around the edges. Let cool on a wire rack. Decorate with store-bought frosting if desired.

Let the children eat the wise man's cookie plain and the foolish man's cookie can be dunked into a white flood (milk).

Lesson 37	Keep the Sabbath Holy

Exodus 20:8

the sa+ 2 ... +p it ... +E

PREPARATION: Review Lesson 37, preparation 3 (p. 199) and discussion activity (p. 200) in the *Primary 2—CTR A* manual.

ACTIVITY:
Sabbath Day Medallion

Create a picture message medallion to strengthen each child's desire to keep the Sabbath Day a holy day. Help children figure out the message and memorize the scripture.

TO MAKE: Using cardstock, copy, color, and cut out the Sabbath medallion that follows for each child. Punch holes at top left and right. Tie a string at each end to hang around child's neck or tell children they can take the medallion home to hang in their room.

THOUGHT TREAT (when appropriate): Sabbath Sandwich. Make a peanut butter or cream cheese sandwich, cutting off the crust; then cut in fourths. Then add the letter "S" for Sunday or Sabbath day on top, using thinned peanut butter or processed cheese in a tube or can.

Lesson 38	Remember Jesus

will ♡ ember sus.   ♡ I will remem Jesu

PREPARATION: Review Lesson 38 and discussions (p. 207-208) in the *Primary 2—CTR A* manual.

ACTIVITY:
Sacrament Reminder Bracelet

This bracelet helps children remember Jesus during the sacrament.

TO MAKE: Using cardstock, copy, color, and cut out the bracelet that follows for each child. Tape or place a 1/2" piece of sticky-back Velcro on bracelet to attach to child's wrist.

THOUGHT TREAT (when appropriate): Unleavened Bread. Provide flat bread or pita bread to show the type of bread Jesus ate; compare it with the yeast breads we often eat today. Explain that the people ate their bread with honey. Serve with honey butter (mix half honey with half butter).

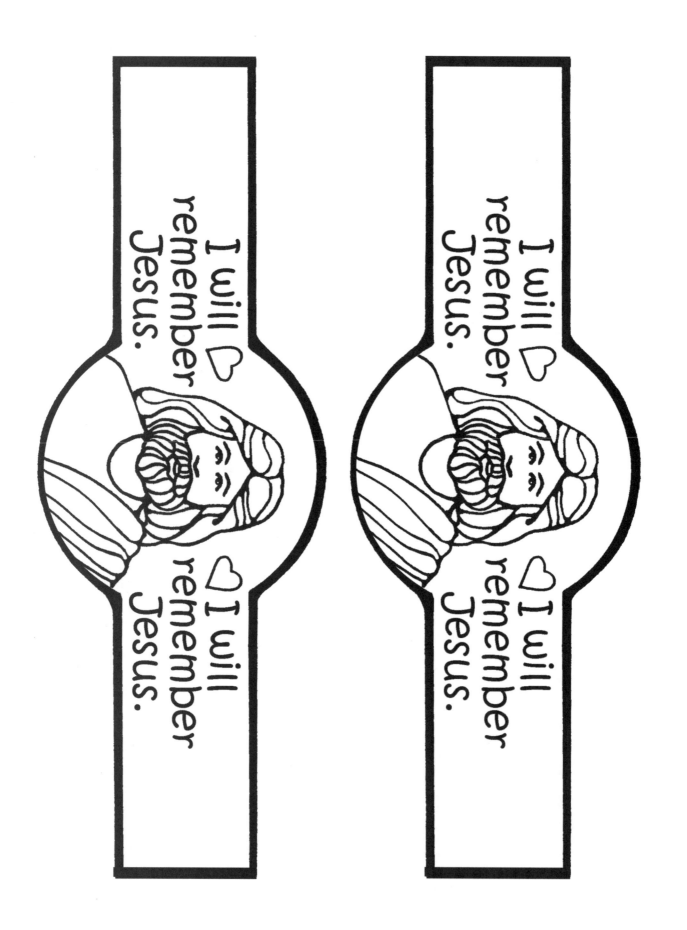

Lesson 39	Serve Others Secretly

PREPARATION: Review Lesson 39 and enrichment activity #2 (p. 215) in the *Primary 2—CTR A* manual

ACTIVITY:
Secret Service Necklace

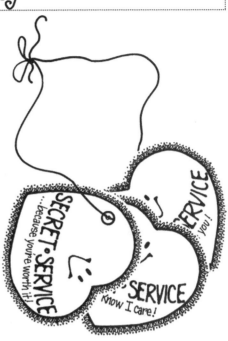

Help children plan secret services they can do for their family and friends. Children can wear this Secret Service Necklace inside their clothes to keep their planned service a secret. When they perform the secret service, they can take a heart off the necklace and leave it for the person to show that someone is secretly serving them.

TO MAKE: Using cardstock, copy, color, and cut out the hearts that follow for each child. Paper punch hearts, then string yarn or ribbon through holes, tying a knot at the end. Place around child's neck.

THOUGHT TREAT (when appropriate): Heart-Shaped Treats. Tell children that each time they help another person secretly, they feel happy in their heart.

Lesson 40	I'm Happy When I Forgive

PREPARATION: Review Lesson 40 and testimony (p. 220) in the *Primary 2—CTR A* manual.

ACTIVITY:
Forgiving Faces

Enjoy opening the situation doors to discover forgiving faces. Help children understand they can be happy when they forgive. Help them open doors to look and talk about the situations and the forgiving face responses.

TO MAKE: Copy, color, and cut out the forgiving faces visuals that follow for each child. Glue situation doors over forgiving faces 1-4.

THOUGHT TREAT (when appropriate): Funny Face Cookies. Decorate round cookies with frosting faces or bake dried fruit faces into the cookie. Tell children that a face can tell us many things. It can tell how a person is feeling and forgiving.

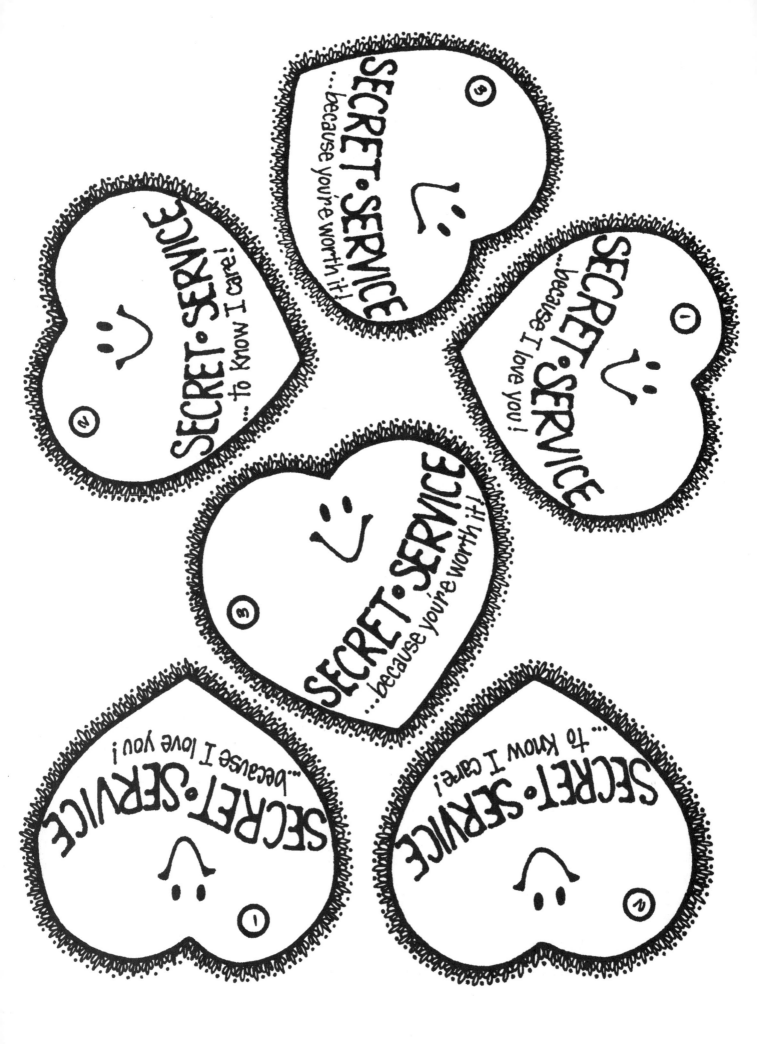

1 | My sister lost my toy!

2 | Someone pushed me down!

3 | Little brother ate my candy!

4 | My friend called me a bad name!

Lesson 41   I Will Be Resurrected

PREPARATION: Review Lesson 41 and enrichment activity #5 (p. 228) in the *Primary 2—CTR A* manual.

ACTIVITY:
Resurrection Glasses

Glasses will show children that because Jesus was resurrected, all can be resurrected again. Even the blind will be able to see again. Wear resurrection glasses as a reminder of this miracle.

TO MAKE: Using cardstock, copy, color, and cut out the resurrection glasses that follow for each child. Glue or tape sides onto glasses to fit child's face.

THOUGHT TREAT (when appropriate): Fresh Fruit or Vegetables. Tell children that after the resurrection, we will have our bodies again. So let's eat these healthy snacks Heavenly Father has created for us.

Lesson 42   Jesus' Church is on the Earth Today

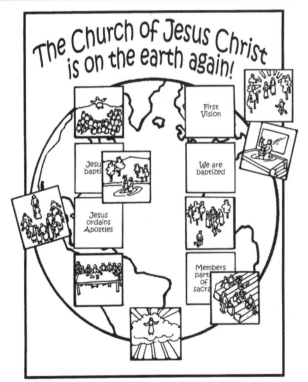

PREPARATION: Review Lesson 42, preparation 4 (p. 229), and teacher presentation (p. 232) in the *Primary 2—CTR A* manual.

ACTIVITY:
Then-and-Now Sticker Poster

This glue-on sticker poster shows: THEN, when the Church of Jesus Christ was originally on the earth and NOW, when it has been restored to the earth again. Stickers show pictures of THEN (when Jesus was on the earth) and NOW (these latter-days).

TO MAKE: Copy, color, and cut out the Then-and-Now poster that follows for each child. Glue stickers on the THEN boxes (on the left) and NOW boxes (on the right). *Option:* Tape pictures on the left or right side so pictures can flap open to see the words.

THOUGHT TREAT (when appropriate): Church House Cookies. See pattern used for Lesson 36 to cut out sugar cookie dough in house shape. Decorate with frosting showing stick figures (people) sitting inside.

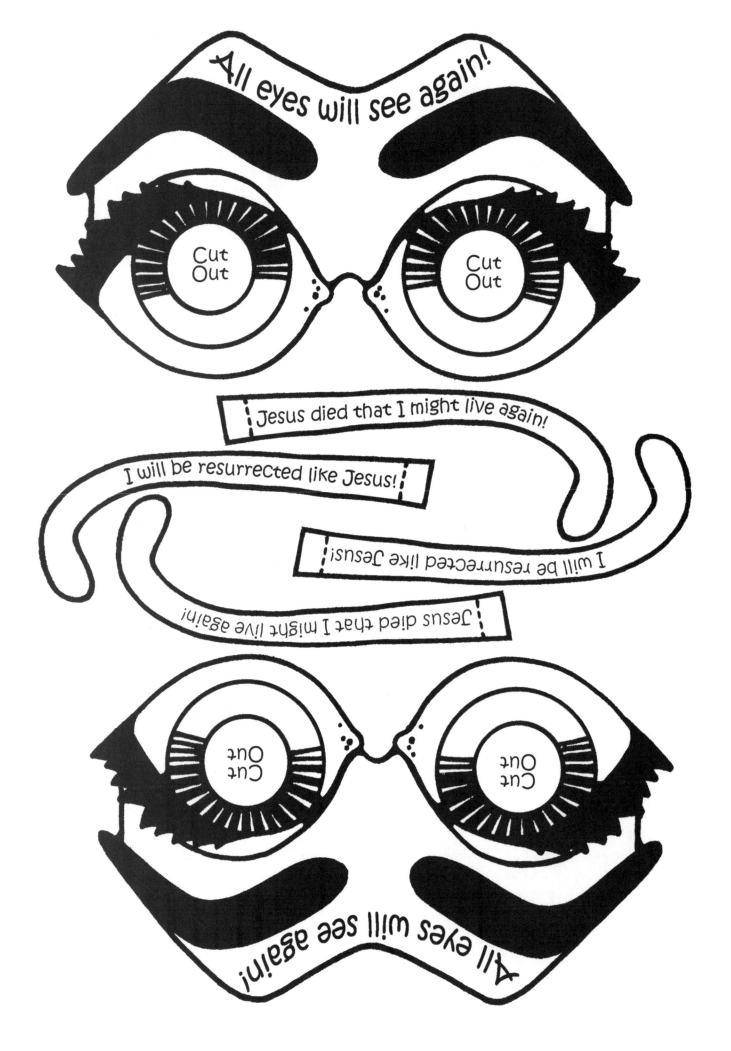

All eyes will see again!

Cut Out

Cut Out

Jesus died that I might live again!

I will be resurrected like Jesus!

I will be resurrected like Jesus!

Jesus died that I might live again!

Cut Out

Cut Out

All eyes will see again!

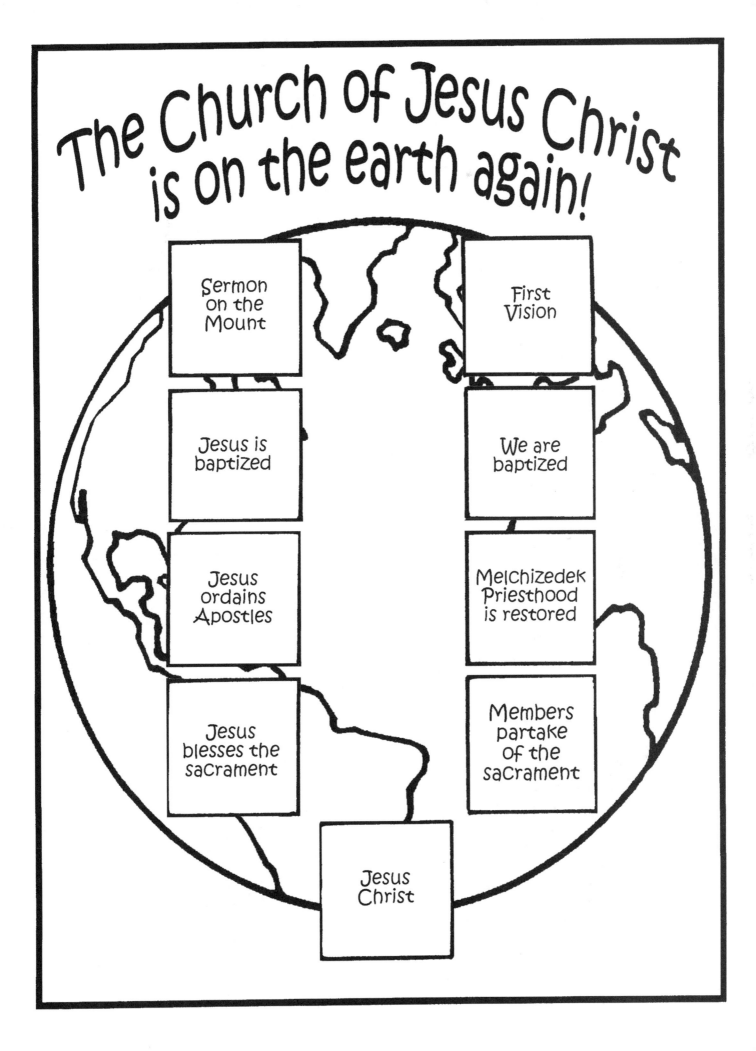

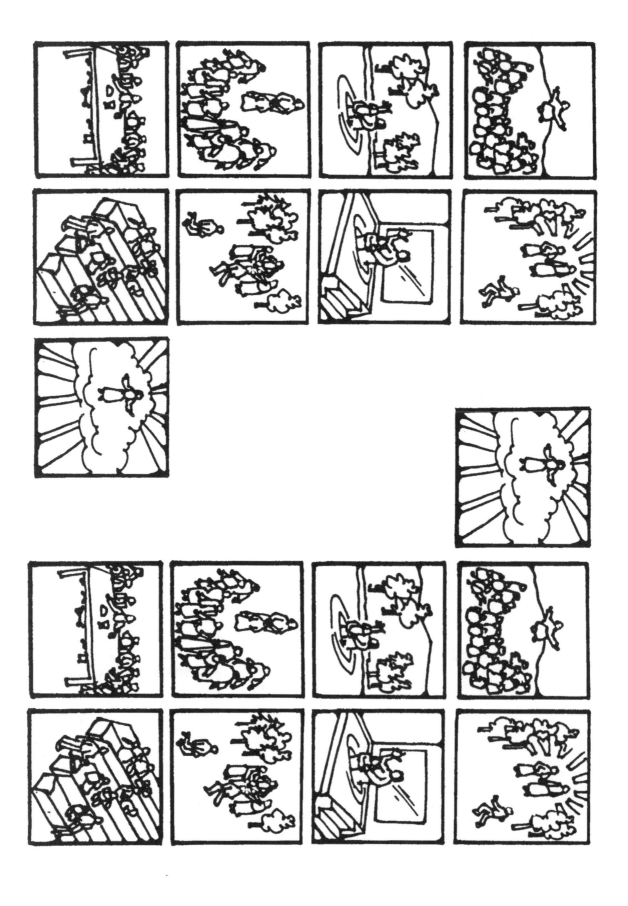

Lesson 43	Be Ready When Jesus Comes Again

PREPARATION: Review Lesson 43 and enrichment activity #4 (p. 239) in the *Primary 2—CTR A* manual.

ACTIVITY:
Second Coming Medallion

This medallion will remind children of the following: On one side, "I am preparing for the Second Coming of Jesus." On the other side, "I Will Keep Heaven in Sight as I Choose the Right."

TO MAKE: Copy, color, and cut out the medallion that follows for each child. Glue medallion parts A and B back-to-back. Punch a hole at the top. Tie yarn or ribbon to fit around child's neck.

THOUGHT TREAT (when appropriate): Eyeglass Cookie (to see your way back to heaven). Roll sugar cookie dough and cut into 2" circles 1/4" thick. Cut a 3/4" hole in the center. Place cut-out cookie on an aluminum foil-covered baking sheet. Crush hard candy and fill in each cookie hole. Bake at 375° for 8–10 minutes. Hard candy melts into glassy appearance. Child can hold cookie to eye and pretend to see to heaven, or to look for Jesus when He comes again.

Lesson 44	Show Love to Every Living Creature

PREPARATION: Review Lesson 44, scripture—Luke 12:16 presentation (p. 241), discussion (p. 242), and testimony (p. 243) in the *Primary 2—CTR A* manual.

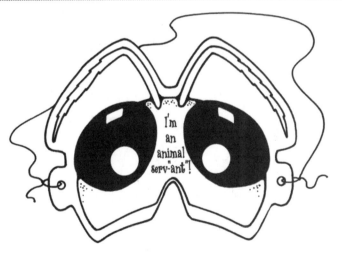

ACTIVITY:
Serv-"ant" Goggles

Children can wear these Serv-"ant" Goggles when they show kindness to every living creature.

TO MAKE: Using cardstock, copy, color, and cut out the goggles that follow for each child. Paper punch holes on sides. Attach yarn or elastic to holes in sides to attach goggles to child's head.

THOUGHT TREAT (when appropriate): Ants on a Log. Cut celery stalks into 3" logs, fill with peanut butter, and top with raisins to resemble ants.

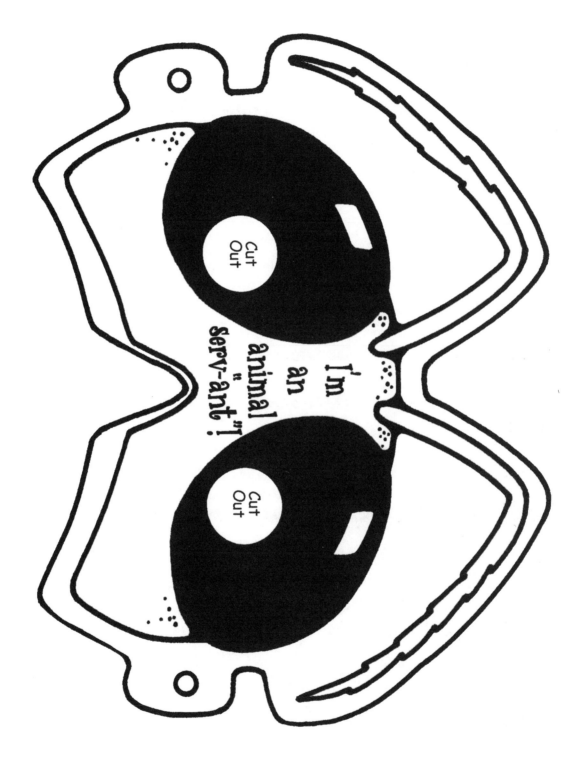

I'm an animal "Serv-ant"!

Cut Out

Cut Out

| Lesson 45 | I Can Be Resurrected Like Jesus |

PREPARATION: Review Lesson 45 and activity (p. 249) in the *Primary 2—CTR A* manual.

ACTIVITY:
Easter Morning Match Game

Play this match game to remind children that we celebrate Easter because Jesus was resurrected. Tell the story using the match cards.

TO PLAY: Turn two sets of cards facedown on table or floor. Children take turns turning two cards over to make a match. If a match is not made, turn cards facedown again in the same place. Each child who makes a match collects matched cards to win.

TO MAKE: Using cardstock, copy, color, and cut out the game that follows for each child, placing each set in a bag to take home.

THOUGHT TREAT (when appropriate): Easter Egg Hunt. Remind children that we like to search for eggs because we are reminded of baby animals born in the spring. It is a new beginning for them. Easter is a new beginning for us. After we die and are resurrected, we receive a new body.

| Lesson 46 | Jesus Is Our Greatest Gift |

PREPARATION: Review Lesson 46, preparation 2 and attention activity (p. 253), and teacher presentation (p. 256) in the *Primary 2—CTR A* manual. *Option:* Create ahead this baby Jesus ornament and place it in the gift box when presenting the Attention activity (p. 253).

ACTIVITY:
3-D Baby Jesus Ornament

Children can proudly hang this ornament on their Christmas tree or in their room to remind them that "Jesus Is Our Greatest Gift."

TO MAKE: Using cardstock, copy, color, and cut out the ornament that follows for each child. *Option:* Before cutting, laminate with contact paper. Fold down tabs and all box sides. Fold baby Jesus center and place inside. Glue side tabs inside box. Fold and glue bow zig-zag line to box zig-zag line. Poke a hole above bow with a pencil and thread a 12" string through to hang on tree.

THOUGHT TREAT (when appropriate): Gift-Wrapped Treats. Tell children that the gift inside is sweet, but the sweetest gift of all is the gift Heavenly Father gave us when He sent His Son Jesus Christ to the earth.

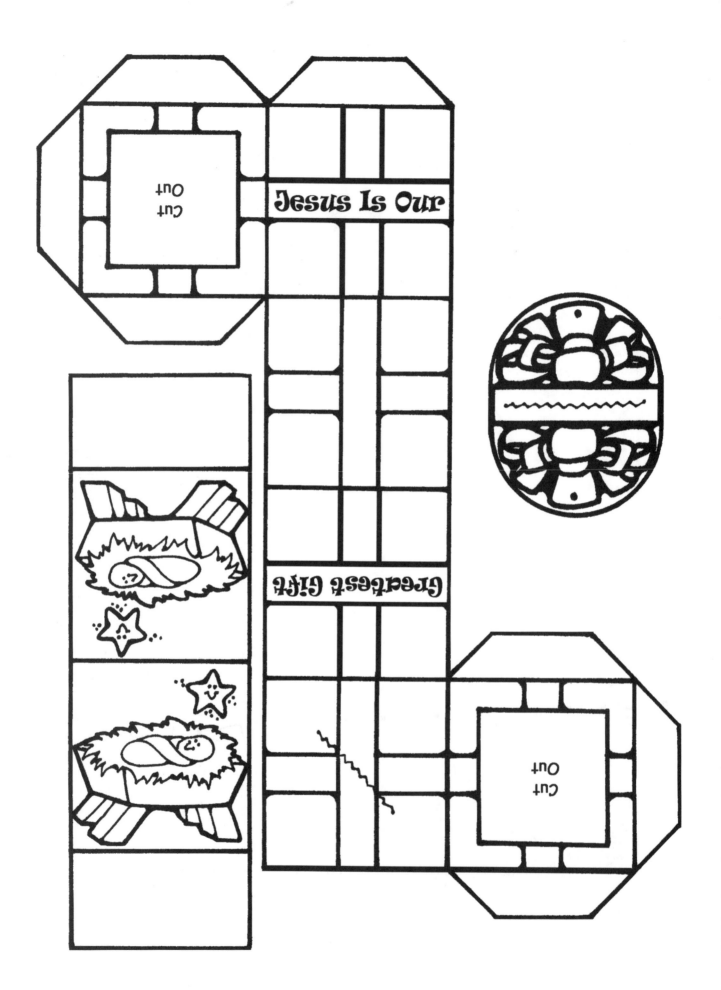

Jesus Is Our

Greatest Gift

Cut Out

Cut Out

Cut Out

Reverence Raccoon Chart

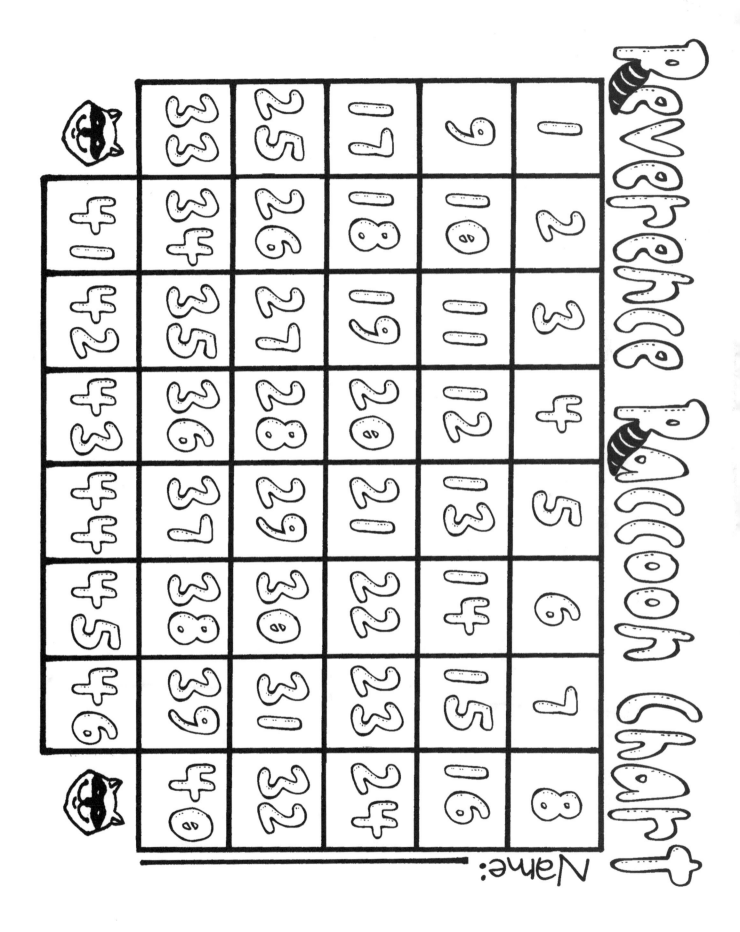

1	2	3	4	5	6	7	8
9	10	11	12	13	14	15	16
17	18	19	20	21	22	23	24
25	26	27	28	29	30	31	32
33	34	35	36	37	38	39	40
	+1	+2	+3	+4	+5	+6	

Name: _____

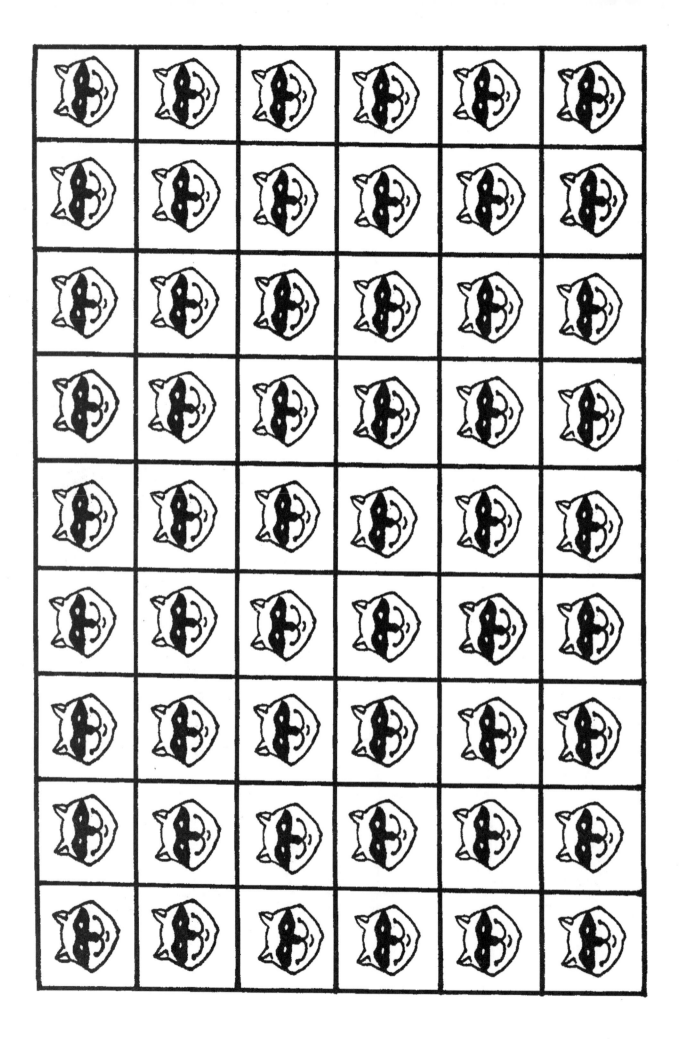

Dear Parents:

This is

_____'s

CTR
Testimony
Treasure Box

Each week, please encourage your child to display the activity creations made in Primary or family home evening.

Children build self-esteem when they show the visuals they have made and relate the lessons they have learned. This also helps reinforce gospel principles.

Then, store testimony treasures in this, their own CTR Testimony Treasure Box.

Thank you.

_____
Primary Teacher